EDIBLE POCKETS FOR EVERY MEAL
DUMPLINGS, TURNOVERS AND PASTIES

Donna Rathmell German

Bristol Publishing Enterprises
San Leandro, California

a nitty gritty® cookbook

© 1997, Bristol Publishing Enterprises, Inc.,
P.O. Box 1737, San Leandro, California, 94577.
World rights reserved. No part of this publication
may be reproduced in any form, nor may it be
stored in a retrieval system, transmitted, or
otherwise copied for public or private use without
prior written permission from the publisher.

Printed in the United States of America.
ISBN 1-55867-164-1

Cover design: Frank J. Paredes
Cover photography: John A. Benson
Food stylist: Susan Massey
Illustrator: James Balkovek

CONTENTS

No book could be written without the support of friends and family,
for which I am very grateful. Many thanks to Kathy Atkinson, Myra Davis,
Shannon Williams and Maria Von Tersch for all their help, tasting, testing and
general moral support. As always, thanks to my three daughters,
Rachel, Katie and Helen, and to my husband, Lee,
for putting up with me when I am stressed to meet a deadline
and for eating their way through the recipes.

ABOUT EDIBLE POCKETS

Whether they are called dumplings, turnovers, pasties, calzones, empanadas, piroshki, boreks, quesadillas, knishes, pot stickers or any other name, edible pockets are enjoyed all over the world. They can be filled with meats, cheeses, fruits or sweets; they can be wrapped with a yeast-leavened dough, pastry dough, or premade wrapper; they can be baked, fried, boiled or steamed. Pockets are so important in some cultures that the baker marks the pocket with a design or even his or her initials before baking. Pockets make wonderful appetizers, picnic fare or light entrées. There is something inherently fun about eating pockets fresh from the oven or even cold from the refrigerator.

It is easy to understand how turnovers became such an integral part of food traditions. Nomads and peasants frequently would not have plates on which to serve or eat food. As a result, foods were often served in edible wrappers or on flatbreads like pizza. Cornish pasties were developed in the 18th century for the tin miners in Cornwall, England, who had to carry their lunch in their pockets.

The basis for pocket wrappers depended on what was grown in the region. For example, many wrappers found in the Americas were made from corn, a staple of the region. Wheat grown in the Middle East served as the basis for edible pockets there.

There are some traditional pockets that use a specific filling, a specific wrapper and are cooked by a specific method. For example, Mexican quesadillas are traditionally made with tortillas, contain savory fillings and are fried or griddled. Turkish boreks use a very thinly rolled pastry dough, a variety of savory fillings and are generally deep fat-fried. Greek spanakopita triangles are made with a phyllo wrapper, contain a spinach and feta filling and are baked or fried. South American empanadas are usually made with pastry dough and a savory or sweet filling and are baked or fried. Cornish pasties are made from pastry dough, use a chopped meat and potato filling and are baked.

This book is divided into recipes for doughs and fillings, which can be mixed and matched as desired. Each dough recipe suggests either a specific filling recipe or general ideas on what type of filling will complement the dough. Each filling recipe lists at least three suggested wrappers, but you are not limited to just the wrappers listed. Use your imagination.

Making flavorful pockets does not have to be a major undertaking. With one or two simple doughs and a few easy fillings, it is possible to have an elegant buffet of pockets for friends or family. The most time-consuming part of pockets is filling the dough. Once you have made them a few times, you'll feel comfortable enough to throw them together without even thinking about it — I promise!

INGREDIENTS

- Cheeses in fillings are usually grated or crumbled for ease. Use a food processor to save time. Or, opt for purchased grated cheeses. Parmesan cheese is best when freshly grated. As an alternative, look for grated Parmesan in plastic tubs (not the green can) in the specialty cheese section of large grocery stores.

- Cream cheese can be regular, light or nonfat.

- Egg whites are used as a wash in the majority of the dough recipes. The remaining egg yolks can be frozen for later use. Gently stir the yolk to break it. To prevent it from becoming gummy, mix in a little salt or sugar. Place the yolk in an ice cube tray and freeze. When frozen completely, place the yolk cube in a locking freezer bag and keep frozen until needed.

- Garlic and ginger root are best when used fresh, but they can be found minced or chopped in jars in the produce section of most grocery stores.

- Meats (beef, chicken, lamb, pork or turkey) are ground in these recipes for ease and should be well cooked before using.

- Herbs can be either fresh or dried, depending on what you have on hand. Crushing dried herbs releases the flavor. I generally drop the measured amount of dried herbs into my hands and crush them between my fingers as I sprinkle them into the filling or dough.

- Jalapeño peppers can be adjusted to taste. Remove the seeds and ribs before chopping for a milder flavor. Substitute any favorite hot chile pepper if desired.

- Nuts are interchangeable if you have an abundance of a particular kind, but note that they do add very specific flavors that will affect the filling. Walnuts and pecans in particular are often substituted for each other. To release the flavor of nuts, cook them in a skillet in a small amount of butter or oil for 2 to 3 minutes over medium-high heat. Remember to stir constantly so they won't burn. In general, nuts should be coarsely chopped — a food processor makes the job quick and easy.

- Onions should be freshly diced or minced. Adjust to taste if desired.

- Tomatoes should be seeded and diced before using in fillings. Plum tomatoes (also called Italian or Roma) work very well. Cut off the stem end and gently squeeze out the juice and seeds. Dice the remaining tomato flesh. Preparing the tomatoes in this manner provides great tomato flavor, yet keeps the filling from becoming too watery.

- Yeast for the yeast dough recipes is the fast-acting (quick-rise or bread machine) variety.

EQUIPMENT

POCKET MAKERS

Also called turnover presses or dumpling presses, these are wonderful gadgets that make professional-looking pockets in a flash. Check the bottom of the press to see if it has a "cutter" that cuts the dough to the proper size. If it doesn't have a cutter, use a biscuit cutter, jar or other round edge to cut dough. With these gadgets, you cut the dough, position the dough on the press, brush the dough with egg wash or a similar ingredient, place the proper amount of filling in the center and squeeze the press to seal the sides of the dough together. Spray the sealing side of the press with nonstick vegetable spray after making 4 or 5 pockets to prevent sticking. Some pocket makers even come in fanciful shapes, such as flowers or hearts.

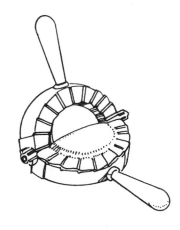

PIEROGI OR RAVIOLI MAKERS

These tools are traditionally used for filled pasta dumplings. Any dough, not just pasta dough, can be used in the same general manner. Pierogi and ravioli makers can be found in specialty gourmet shops and mail-order catalogs. They have two parts: one that forms the outline of the pockets and serves as the cutting edge, and one that makes indentations in the dough into which the filling will rest. Pierogi makers make half-moon shaped pockets, and ravioli makers make square pockets.

Divide yeast doughs into 4 to 6 pieces; divide pastry doughs into 4 to 5 pieces. Roll each piece into 2 long, thin sheets, just longer than the pierogi or ravioli maker. Lay one of the sheets of dough over the cutting plate, leaving extra dough hanging over the edges, and brush the dough with egg wash. Press the shaping plate into the dough gently to make small indentations. Place a teaspoon of filling into each indentation. Cover the filled dough with the second sheet of dough. With a rolling pin, roll the dough firmly from the center outwards. This will both seal and cut the pockets. Spray the pierogi maker with nonstick vegetable spray as necessary while making pockets.

CUTTING AND SEALING GADGETS

These items come in many forms. Some make round pockets, some make square pockets and some make pockets of any shape, depending on how you cut the pastry. One type is often called a ravioli cutter, and consists of a square or round graduated cutting shape that is attached to a wooden handle. Another variety is sometimes called a pastry crimper, and consists of a perforated metal wheel attached to a long wooden handle. Another specialized type consists of a sealing plate and a spring-loaded handle. In any case, the procedure for making pockets is essentially the same.

Divide doughs into 4 to 6 pieces and roll each piece into 2 long, thin rectangles. Place teaspoons of filling on top of 1 sheet of dough and place another sheet of dough on top. Center the gadget on top of the filling and press down firmly on the dough to cut and seal it at the same time. For some gadgets, you may have to twist lightly. For a pastry crimper, roll it across the dough in the desired shape. Straight lines work best with this gadget. When using these gadgets, it takes some practice to get the spacing of the filling correct, but is relatively easy once you get the hang of it.

SIMPLE PAIRINGS

Pairing doughs with fillings is so easy, you don't even need a recipe. Here are some quick and easy ideas.

- *Tomato Basil Yeast Dough*, page 22, *Garlic Herb Yeast Dough*, page 24, or *Basic Savory Pastry Dough* with herbs, page 36, pair nicely with any of the following choices: a slice of cheddar, mozzarella or any favorite cheese; a slice each of proscuitto and mozzarella cheese; a slice each of feta cheese and tomato and a basil leaf; a slice each of pepperoni and mozzarella cheese; a small amount of cooked chorizo or kielbasa; a spoonful of herbed cheese spread; a slice of goat cheese with or without a slice of Roma tomato.

- *Basic Sweet Yeast Dough*, page 16, *Basic Sweet Pastry Dough*, page 37, or *Pie Crust*, page 52, are great filled with one of the following choices: hazelnut chocolate sauce, such as Nutella; chopped pitted dates and/or chopped nuts; guava paste alone or with a little cream cheese; cream cheese mixed with preserves; canned pie filling, pureed if desired; small pieces of Brie cheese with or without a little fresh chopped basil.

LEFTOVERS

If you have leftovers sitting in your refrigerator, try using them as pocket fillings. Many leftovers can simply be thrown in the food processor to produce a filling. However, try not to use high-moisture fillings, as they tend to leak out of the dough during baking.

LEFTOVER DOUGH

- Leftover yeast dough can be shaped into small rolls and allowed to rise for 30 to 40 minutes. Brush the top with egg wash and bake for about 15 to 18 minutes until golden brown.
- Leftover pastry dough is wonderful rolled out, brushed with melted butter, sprinkled with cinnamon sugar and baked for 10 to 14 minutes.

LEFTOVER FILLING

- Put it in a plastic bag, label and freeze it to use on a later day.
- Toss leftover cheese or meat fillings into scrambled eggs or mix with hot cooked rice.
- Spread meat fillings, bean fillings, or sweet or savory cheese fillings on toast.

YEAST DOUGH WRAPPERS

ABOUT YEAST DOUGHS

Whether you make yeast dough by hand or in a machine, get to know the feel and look of the dough. It should always come together in a round ball, but not be sticky to the touch. Adjust the dough during kneading if necessary by adding a tablespoon of water or flour at a time until the dough reaches the proper consistency. Flour absorbs moisture as it sits on the shelf, so it often requires minor adjustments. The more moist the dough, the more tender the wrapper will be. Add flour sparingly —just enough so that the dough handles easily. All yeast dough recipes were tested using a fast-acting (quick or bread machine) yeast. If you make these recipes with a food processor or by hand, the ingredients will not appear in order.

GENERAL INSTRUCTIONS FOR MAKING YEAST DOUGH POCKETS

1. Make dough.

Bread Machine: Warm liquids to lukewarm (baby bottle temperature). Add ingredients to the bread machine pan in the order specified by the manufacturer. Use the dough (manual) cycle to knead the dough and to allow it to rise once. It is not necessary to let the dough rise for more than 1 hour. If your machine has a double-kneading dough cycle (DAK and Welbilt ABM 100), remove the dough after an hour or so and turn off your machine. Allowing the dough to knead the second time causes air bubbles that makes the dough difficult to roll.

Food Processor: Warm liquids to lukewarm (baby bottle temperature). Combine dry ingredients, including yeast, in the workbowl; process for 10 seconds. Mix remaining ingredients together and pour through the feed tube until the dough forms a ball. If the dough feels sticky, add flour 1 tablespoon at a time until dough is smooth. Process dough for about 1 minute, or knead dough by hand for about 5 to 10 minutes. Shape dough into a ball, place in a greased bowl and cover with a kitchen towel. Place bowl in a warm, draft-free location and let dough rise for 30 to 45 minutes, until doubled in size.

By Hand: In a bowl, mix yeast with flour. Mix together liquid ingredients and add to flour mixture, stirring well. Add all other ingredients and stir together until you can no longer work the dough with a spoon. Transfer the dough to a lightly floured work surface, scraping the bowl well. Pat the dough into a ball and flatten it slightly. With the heels of your hands, knead the dough until it is smooth and not sticky, adding flour 1 tablespoon at a time if necessary; continue kneading for 5 to 10 minutes. Shape dough into a ball, place in a greased bowl and cover with a kitchen towel. Place bowl in a warm, draft-free location and let rise for 30 to 45 minutes, until doubled in size.

2. While the yeast dough is rising, make the filling according to the directions in the recipe of your choice.

3. Prepare an egg wash by mixing 1 beaten egg white with 1 to 2 tablespoons water.

4. Preheat oven to 375° unless otherwise specified.

5. Grease a baking sheet with vegetable oil, spray it with nonstick vegetable spray or line it with parchment paper.

6. On a lightly floured work surface, roll the dough as thinly as possible, about $1/8$ inch. Let the dough rest for about 5 minutes. With a turnover press or a round cutter, cut the dough into circles. Yeast doughs have a tendency to shrink slightly after they are cut. Stretch the dough into shape if necessary.

7. Brush the dough circles lightly with egg wash, which serves as glue for the dough when it is pressed together. If you are using a turnover press, place the dough circles into the press before brushing with egg wash.

8. Place desired filling in the center of each dough circle. Fold each circle in half and press firmly your fingers, the tines of a fork or the handles of the turnover press to seal the dough well. It is helpful to spray the turnover press, if using, with nonstick vegetable spray every few times to prevent the dough from sticking to the press.

- Fill each 2-inch pocket with $\frac{1}{2}$ teaspoon filling.
  One cup filling fills about 96 pockets.

- Fill each 3-inch pocket with 1 to $1\frac{1}{2}$ teaspoons filling.
  One cup filling fills 36 to 48 pockets.

- Fill each 4-inch pocket with 2 teaspoons to $1\frac{1}{2}$ tablespoons filling.
  One cup filling fills 24 to 32 pockets.

- Fill each 6-inch pocket with 3 tablespoons to $\frac{1}{2}$ cup filling.
  One cup filling fills 2 to 5 pockets.

- Fill each 8-inch pocket with $\frac{1}{2}$ to $\frac{3}{4}$ cup filling.
  One cup filling fills 2 pockets.

BAKING YEAST DOUGH POCKETS

Filled yeast-dough pockets can be baked immediately for a chewy, less "bready" crust, or allowed to rise for a short time for a thicker crust that's light in texture. If you opt for the latter, cover pockets with a kitchen towel and let rise in a warm, draft-free location for 20 to 30 minutes. If the edges of the pockets separate during rising, press them back together with your fingers. Brush with egg wash or olive oil to provide a glossy sheen. Bake filled pockets for 15 to 20 minutes until golden brown.

If not baking immediately after filling, do not brush yeast dough pockets with egg wash or olive oil. Cover filled pockets lightly with plastic wrap and refrigerate for up to 24 hours. The dough will rise slightly. When ready to bake, remove pockets from the refrigerator, brush with egg wash or olive oil and bake for a few minutes longer than called for.

Yeast dough pockets can also be assembled (do not use a wash), wrapped tightly and frozen for up to 2 months. To bake, remove pockets from the freezer, thaw in the refrigerator overnight (or all day), brush with egg wash or olive oil and bake for a few minutes longer than called for.

To warm baked yeast dough pockets, wrap in aluminum foil and bake in a preheated 350° oven until warm throughout, about 5 minutes.

Serve yeast dough pockets warm, or cool on a wire rack and serve at room temperature.

BASIC SAVORY YEAST DOUGH

Any combination of meat or cheese fillings can be used with this basic yeast dough. This is a great dough to use for wrapping up various leftovers in the refrigerator. Each and every filling in this book can be made into a pocket with this versatile dough.

1 cup water
2 tbs. olive or canola oil
1 tsp. sugar
½ tsp. salt
3 cups unbleached all-purpose flour
1½ tsp. fast-acting yeast

Preheat oven to 375°. Bake filled pockets for 15 to 20 minutes until golden brown.

SUGGESTED SIZES AND YIELDS

2-inch pockets: makes 46-48   **6-inch pockets: makes 5-6**
3-inch pockets: makes 24-36   **8-inch pockets: makes 4-5**
4-inch pockets: makes 20-23

BASIC SWEET YEAST DOUGH

Use cinnamon to bring out the flavor of a specific filling. Substitute nutmeg, grated orange peel or lemon peel if desired. This dough makes wonderful breakfast or dessert treats with nut, sweet cheese or fruit fillings. If making the dough by hand or with a food processor, melt the butter and cool it slightly before adding it to the flour mixture.

1⅛ cups milk
3 tbs. butter or margarine
2 tbs. sugar
½ tsp. salt

1 tsp. cinnamon, optional
3 cups unbleached all-purpose flour
1½ tsp. fast-acting yeast

Preheat oven to 350°. Bake filled pockets for 15 to 20 minutes until golden brown.

SUGGESTED SIZES AND YIELDS
2-inch pockets: makes 46-48
3-inch pockets: makes 24-36
4-inch pockets: makes 20-23

6-inch pockets: makes 5-6
8-inch pockets: makes 4-5

POTATO YEAST DOUGH

This yeasted potato dough gives the flavor of a Middle Eastern potato dumpling. The dough is easy to roll and press. Save the water in which the potatoes were cooked for the dough. If making the dough by hand or with a food processor, melt the butter, cool it slightly and mix it with the mashed potatoes and water. For a sweet treat, make small pockets with a halved (or quartered) apricot inside. Serve them as is or with a fruit syrup or honey butter. If you desire a savory pocket, you can use virtually any cheese, onion or meat filling. Cheddar cheese is especially good with this dough.

$^1/_2$ cup mashed potatoes
$^3/_4$ cup potato water
1 tbs. butter or margarine
$^1/_4$ tsp. salt

$^1/_4$ tsp. pepper
3 cups unbleached all-purpose flour
$1^1/_2$ tsp. fast-acting yeast

Preheat oven to 375°. Bake filled pockets for 15 to 20 minutes until golden brown.

SUGGESTED SIZES AND YIELDS
2-inch pockets: makes 46-48
3-inch pockets: makes 24-36
4-inch pockets: makes 20-23

6-inch pockets: makes 5-6
8-inch pockets: makes 4-5

RYE YEAST DOUGH

People always rave about the pockets made with this unique dough. Just about any sandwich filling you enjoy on rye bread can be used. Fill rye pockets with equal amounts of diced ham and shredded cheese. For even more flavor, coat the inside of the pockets with mustard instead of egg wash. Another delicious and simple filling is nothing more than chopped onions and shredded cheddar cheese.

1 cup water
2 tbs. vegetable oil
2 tbs. molasses
1 tsp. salt
1 tbs. cocoa powder

1 tbs. caraway seeds, optional
½ cup instant potato flakes
1 cup rye flour
2 cups unbleached all-purpose flour
2 tsp. fast-acting yeast

Preheat oven to 375°. Bake filled pockets for 15 to 20 minutes until golden brown.

SUGGESTED SIZES AND YIELDS
2-inch pockets: makes 44-46
3-inch pockets: makes 22-34
4-inch pockets: makes 18-21

6-inch pockets: makes 4-5
8-inch pockets: makes 3-4

WHOLE WHEAT YEAST DOUGH

This dough will make a smaller number of pockets than a recipe using all-purpose flour. The dough is flavorful, healthy and low-rising, and can be used for any savory cheese or meat filling.

1 cup water
2 tbs. canola or vegetable oil
1 tbs. honey
½ tsp. salt
3 cups whole wheat flour
2 tsp. fast-acting yeast

Preheat oven to 375°. Bake filled pockets for 15 to 20 minutes until golden brown.

SUGGESTED SIZES AND YIELDS
2-inch pockets: makes 44-46
3-inch pockets: makes 22-24
4-inch pockets: makes 18-20

6-inch pockets: makes 4-5
8-inch pockets: makes 3-4

MEXICAN YEAST DOUGH

Masa harina, which literally means "dough flour" in Spanish, is found in many large grocery stores in the Mexican section. It can be called "maseca." For this flour, corn is soaked in a lime solution, dried and ground, which gives it that special flavor. A good-quality stone-ground cornmeal can be substituted if masa harina is unavailable. Fill pockets with any basic cheese or taco-style filling.

1 cup water
2 tbs. vegetable or canola oil
½-1 diced jalapeño pepper, optional
1 tbs. sugar
½ tsp. salt

½ cup masa harina or stone-ground cornmeal
2½ cups unbleached all-purpose flour
1½ tsp. fast-acting yeast

Preheat oven to 375°. Bake filled pockets for 15 to 20 minutes until golden brown.

SUGGESTED SIZES AND YIELDS
2-inch pockets: makes 46-48
3-inch pockets: makes 24-36
4-inch pockets: makes 20-23

6-inch pockets: makes 5-6
8-inch pockets: makes 4-5

TOMATO BASIL YEAST DOUGH

If you make tomato juice by hand, add ½ tsp. salt. Purchased tomato juice already contains enough salt. Lamb fillings go nicely with this dough. Italian and Middle Eastern-flavored cheese or meat fillings also work well. Substitute mint for basil if desired.

1⅛ cups tomato juice
2 tbs. olive oil
1 tsp. sugar
3 tbs. chopped fresh basil, or 1 tbs. dried, crushed
3 cups unbleached all-purpose flour
1½ tsp. fast-acting yeast

Preheat oven to 375°. Bake filled pockets for 15 to 20 minutes until golden brown.

SUGGESTED SIZES AND YIELDS

2-inch pockets: makes 46-48	**6-inch pockets: makes 5-6**
3-inch pockets: makes 24-36	**8-inch pockets: makes 4-5**
4-inch pockets: makes 20-23	

GARLIC YEAST DOUGH

This savory dough complements just about any meat filling. It is a wonderful choice when using leftovers as filling ingredients.

1 cup water
2 tbs. olive oil
2 cloves garlic, minced
1 tsp. sugar
½ tsp. salt
3 cups unbleached all-purpose flour
1½ tsp. fast-acting yeast

Preheat oven to 375°. Bake filled pockets for 15 to 20 minutes until golden brown.

SUGGESTED SIZES AND YIELDS
2-inch pockets: makes 46-48
3-inch pockets: makes 24-36
4-inch pockets: makes 20-23

6-inch pockets: makes 5-6
8-inch pockets: makes 4-5

GARLIC HERB YEAST DOUGH

Use any herb, such as basil, parsley, oregano, cilantro, mint, tarragon or dill, to complement your chosen filling. The herbs can be adjusted to taste. This basic dough can be used with virtually any meat or cheese filling.

1 cup water
2 tbs. olive oil
2 cloves garlic, minced
$\frac{1}{2}$ tsp. salt
3 tbs. chopped fresh herbs, or 1 tbs. dried, crushed
3 cups unbleached all-purpose flour
$1\frac{1}{2}$ tsp. fast-acting yeast

Preheat oven to 375°. Bake filled pockets for 15 to 20 minutes until golden brown.

SUGGESTED SIZES AND YIELDS

2-inch pockets: makes 46-48
3-inch pockets: makes 24-36
4-inch pockets: makes 20-23

6-inch pockets: makes 5-6
8-inch pockets: makes 4-5

ONION YEAST DOUGH

The moisture of this dough is very much affected by the freshness of the onion used. If kneading by machine, check the consistency of the dough after 5 minutes and adjust the dough with water or flour. If kneading by hand, you may need to add a little more water. Use this dough with sharp cheddar cheese, ham and cheese or any other meat fillings.

¾ cup water
¼ cup minced onion
2 tbs. olive oil
½ tsp. salt
3 cups unbleached all-purpose flour
1½ tsp. fast-acting yeast

Preheat oven to 375°. Bake filled pockets for 15 to 20 minutes until golden brown.

SUGGESTED SIZES AND YIELDS

2-inch pockets: makes 46-48
3-inch pockets: makes 24-36
4-inch pockets: makes 20-23

6-inch pockets: makes 5-6
8-inch pockets: makes 4-5

LEMON MINT YEAST DOUGH

This is one of my favorite doughs. It is very flavorful and complements many different types of fillings. I love using this with feta cheese or lamb fillings.

⅞ cup water
3 tbs. lemon juice
1 tbs. olive oil
½ tsp. salt
1 tsp. lemon pepper seasoning
3 tbs. chopped fresh mint, or 1 tbs. dried, crushed
3 cups unbleached all-purpose flour
1½ tsp. fast-acting yeast

Preheat oven to 375°. Bake filled pockets for 15 to 20 minutes until golden brown.

SUGGESTED SIZES AND YIELDS

2-inch pockets: makes 46-48
3-inch pockets: makes 24-36
4-inch pockets: makes 20-23

6-inch pockets: makes 5-6
8-inch pockets: makes 4-5

PARMESAN PEPPER YEAST DOUGH

Use freshly grated Parmesan cheese. Grate it yourself, or purchase it from the produce or cheese sections of the grocery store. Don't use cheese from the green can for this. Almost any cheese filling will complement this dough as will many meat fillings — especially Italian-flavored fillings.

1 cup water
2 tbs. olive or canola oil
½ tsp. salt
1 tsp. coarsely ground pepper
½ cup freshly grated Parmesan cheese

1 tbs. chopped fresh parsley, or 1 tsp.
   dried, crushed, optional
3 cups unbleached all-purpose flour
1½ tsp. fast-acting yeast

Preheat oven to 375°. Bake filled pockets for 15 to 20 minutes until golden brown.

SUGGESTED SIZES AND YIELDS
2-inch pockets: makes 46-48
3-inch pockets: makes 24-36
4-inch pockets: makes 20-23

6-inch pockets: makes 5-6
8-inch pockets: makes 4-5

SPINACH YEAST DOUGH

*Using spinach as the major liquid contributor to a dough can be tricky until you get the feel for it. Adjust the dough's consistency with water or flour as needed only after a full 10 minutes of kneading. Cheese fillings, such as **White Pizza Filling**, page 111, or any lamb-based fillings, go nicely with this dough.*

1 pkg. (10 oz.) frozen chopped spinach, thawed
1 tbs. olive or canola oil
1 clove garlic, minced
1 tsp. sugar
$\frac{1}{2}$ tsp. salt
3 cups unbleached all-purpose flour
$1\frac{1}{2}$ tsp. fast-acting yeast

Preheat oven to 375°. Bake filled pockets for 15 to 20 minutes until golden brown.

SUGGESTED SIZES AND YIELDS
2-inch pockets: makes 46-48
3-inch pockets: makes 24-36
4-inch pockets: makes 20-23

6-inch pockets: makes 5-6
8-inch pockets: makes 4-5

ORANGE GINGER YEAST DOUGH

*Dried ginger powder just doesn't give this filling the right flavor. Use either freshly grated ginger root or minced ginger root found in jars in the produce section of your grocery store. Use either sweet or savory fillings for this dough, such as **Sweet Cheese Filling**, page 142, or **Moroccan Chicken Filling**, page 64. Use 2-inch dough circles to enclose a single cranberry that has been rolled in sugar. It's a great holiday appetizer idea. A dried cherry or sweetened dried cranberry (craisin) is a good substitute for the fresh cranberry.*

1⅛ cups orange juice
2 tbs. sesame oil
1 tsp. freshly grated ginger root

½ tsp. salt
3 cups unbleached all-purpose flour
1½ tsp. fast-acting yeast

Preheat oven to 375°. Bake filled pockets for 15 to 20 minutes until golden brown.

SUGGESTED SIZES AND YIELDS
2-inch pockets: makes 46-48
3-inch pockets: makes 24-36
4-inch pockets: makes 20-23

6-inch pockets: makes 5-6
8-inch pockets: makes 4-5

PASTRY DOUGH WRAPPERS

ABOUT PASTRY DOUGH

Making good pastry dough takes patience and practice. It may take several attempts before you are satisfied with the results. Unlike yeast doughs, which require warm liquids, the colder the liquids, as well as the flour, butter and shortening, the better the pastry dough will be.

A pastry dough's flakiness comes from cutting the shortening and butter into the dry ingredients. For best results, use a pastry blender or two knives to mix the dough. You can use your fingers, but the warmth from your hands may cause the pastry to be tough. Do not use a butter substitute in these recipes.

When adding liquids, add only enough to hold the dough together when it is pressed gently. Take extra care not to overmix pastry dough or to add too much liquid.

Chilling pastry dough is an important step. Keep unused dough refrigerated until needed. If the dough warms up too much, wrap it in plastic and refrigerate until chilled, about 5 to 10 minutes.

When rolling the dough, use only enough flour to prevent sticking. Too much flour will toughen the dough. Using a pastry cloth, plastic pastry sheet or plastic wrap reduces the amount of surplus flour needed. Use a good heavy-duty rolling pin to make the job a lot easier. Roll the dough from the center towards the outside edge. You should actually see pieces of butter in the dough while rolling. It is these layers of butter that cause the dough to flake.

GENERAL INSTRUCTIONS FOR MAKING PASTRY DOUGH POCKETS

1. Make dough.

Food Processor: In the workbowl, combine dry ingredients and dry flavorings (such as grated citrus peel, flaked coconut or minced ginger root). Add shortening and butter and process with very quick pulses until crumbs are the size of a pea. Mix together liquid ingredients (eggs, vinegar, lemon juice, flavoring extracts and ice water) until well blended. With the machine running, slowly pour the liquid mixture through the feed tube until dough just starts to hold together. Discard unused liquids.

By Hand: In a large bowl, combine dry ingredients and dry flavorings (such as grated citrus peel, flaked coconut or minced ginger root). With a pastry blender or two knives, cut shortening into dry ingredients until it resembles coarse meal. Cut in butter until crumbs are the size of a pea. Mix together liquid ingredients (eggs, vinegar, lemon juice, flavoring extracts and ice water) until well blended. Sprinkle liquid mixture, 1 tablespoon at a time, over crumb mixture and toss mixture together with a fork until just moistened. Dough should be just moist enough to hold together. Discard unused liquids.

2. Remove dough from the bowl, bringing it together with your hands. Divide dough into three equal portions and press each portion into a disk. Wrap each disk tightly in plastic. Refrigerate pastry dough for at least 30 minutes or overnight.

3. While the pastry dough is chilling, make the filling according to the directions in the recipe of your choice.

4. Unless otherwise specified in the dough recipe, prepare an egg wash by mixing 1 beaten egg white with 1 to 2 tablespoons water.

5. Preheat oven to 400° unless otherwise specified.

6. If indicated in the dough recipe, grease a baking sheet with olive oil, spray it with nonstick vegetable spray or line it with parchment paper. In general, pastry dough pockets can be baked on ungreased baking sheets.

7. Remove the dough from the refrigerator and let sit at room temperature until pliable, about 5 to 15 minutes. Place dough on a very lightly floured work surface and place a sheet of plastic wrap on top of the dough. Roll the dough as thinly as possible, about $\frac{1}{8}$ inch. With a turnover press or round cutter, cut the dough into circles.

8. Brush the dough circles lightly with egg wash, which serves as glue for the dough when it is pressed together. If you are using a turnover press, place the dough circles into the press before brushing with egg wash.

9. Place desired filling in the center of each dough circle. Fold each circle in half and press firmly with your fingers, the tines of a fork or the handles of a turnover press to seal the dough well. It is helpful to spray the turnover press, if using, with non-stick vegetable spray every few times to prevent the dough from sticking to the press.

- Fill each 2-inch pocket with ½ teaspoon filling.
  One cup filling fills about 96 pockets.
- Fill each 3-inch pocket with 1 to 1½ teaspoons filling.
  One cup filling fills 36 to 48 pockets.
- Fill each 4-inch pocket with 2 teaspoons to 1½ tablespoons filling.
  One cup filling fills 24 to 32 pockets.
- Fill each 6-inch pocket with 3 tablespoons to ½ cup filling.
  One cup filling fills 2 to 5 pockets.

- Fill each 8-inch pocket with ½ to ¾ cup filling.
  One cup filling fills 2 pockets.

BAKING PASTRY DOUGH POCKETS

Place filled pockets on a baking sheet. Brush tops with egg wash to provide a glossy sheen. Bake pockets as directed in recipe.

If not baking immediately, do not brush pastry pockets with egg wash. Cover filled pockets with plastic wrap and refrigerate for up to 8 hours. When ready to bake, remove pockets from the refrigerator, brush with egg wash and bake for a few minutes longer than called for.

Pastry dough pockets can also be assembled (do not use a wash), frozen on a baking sheet, placed in a locking plastic bag and frozen for 2 to 3 weeks. To bake, place frozen pockets on a baking sheet, brush with egg wash and bake for a few minutes longer than called for.

To warm baked pastry dough pockets, wrap in aluminum foil and bake in a preheated 350° oven until warm throughout, about 5 to 8 minutes.

Serve pastry dough pockets warm, or cool on a wire rack and serve at room temperature.

BASIC SAVORY PASTRY DOUGH

Pastry dough is used all over the world with sweet fillings, as well as with savory fillings of meat and cheese. For meat fillings, you can add 1 to 2 tsp. coarsely ground pepper or dried herbs to the dry ingredients if desired. Use butter, not margarine, for best results.

3 cups unbleached all-purpose flour
$\frac{1}{2}$ tsp. salt
$\frac{1}{4}$ cup shortening
$\frac{1}{2}$ cup chilled butter, cut into pieces
1 egg
1 tbs. white vinegar
$\frac{1}{2}$ cup ice water

Preheat oven to 400°. Bake filled pockets for 12 to 18 minutes.

SUGGESTED SIZES AND YIELDS
3-inch pockets: makes 25-30
4-inch pockets: makes 12-18

6-inch pockets: makes 5-6

BASIC SWEET PASTRY DOUGH

Use cinnamon or orange peel to complement any sweet cheese or fruit filling.

3 cups unbleached all-purpose flour
½ tsp. salt
1 tbs. sugar
1-2 tsp. cinnamon or grated orange peel, optional
¼ cup shortening
½ cup chilled butter, cut into pieces
1 egg
1 tbs. lemon juice
½ cup ice water

Preheat oven to 400°. Bake filled pockets for 12 to 18 minutes.

SUGGESTED SIZES AND YIELDS
3-inch pockets: makes 25-30
4-inch pockets: makes 12-18

6-inch pockets: makes 5-6

COCONUT GINGER PASTRY DOUGH

Any lemon, nut or tropical-flavored filling goes nicely with this pastry dough. For a delicious, yet very easy turnover, fill this dough with a single maraschino cherry. I prefer using the 3-inch size for this; smaller sizes make it difficult to seal the cherry completely.

3 cups unbleached all-purpose flour
½ tsp. salt
½ cup sweetened flaked coconut
½-1 tsp. grated ginger root
¼ cup shortening

½ cup chilled butter, cut into pieces
1 egg
1 tsp. coconut extract
1 tbs. lemon juice
½ cup ice water

Preheat oven to 400°. Bake filled pockets for 12 to 18 minutes.

SUGGESTED SIZES AND YIELDS
3-inch pockets: makes 25-30
4-inch pockets: makes 12-18

6-inch pockets: makes 5-6

LEMON POPPY SEED PASTRY DOUGH

This versatile dough complements both sweet and savory fillings. Try any sweet filling with almonds, **Herbed Feta Filling** *with mint, page 105, or* **Spanakopita Filling**, *page 119. If using fresh lemon peel (zest), use 2 medium lemons.*

3 cups unbleached all-purpose flour
2 tbs. poppy seeds
1/2 tsp. salt
1 tbs. sugar
1 tbs. grated lemon peel
1/4 cup shortening

1/2 cup chilled butter, cut into pieces
1 egg
1 tsp. lemon extract
1 tbs. lemon juice
1/2 cup ice water

Preheat oven to 400°. Bake filled pockets for 12 to 18 minutes.

SUGGESTED SIZES AND YIELDS
3-inch pockets: makes 25-30
4-inch pockets: makes 12-18

6-inch pockets: makes 5-6

VIENNA PASTRY DOUGH

If using unsalted butter, add ½ tsp. salt to the flour. This basic dough can be used with any filling, sweet or savory.

3 cups unbleached all-purpose flour
1½ cups chilled butter, cut into pieces
1-1½ cups sour cream

Place flour in a large bowl. With a pastry blender, two knives or your fingers, cut in butter until mixture resembles coarse meal. Add 1 cup sour cream and blend until dough holds together without being too sticky. If necessary, add more sour cream, 1 to 2 tablespoons at a time, until dough holds together. Remove dough from bowl, bringing it together with your hands. Divide dough into 3 equal portions and press each portion into a disk. Wrap each disk tightly in plastic. Refrigerate for at least 12 hours.

Preheat oven to 400°. Bake filled pockets for 10 to 15 minutes.

SUGGESTED SIZES AND YIELDS
2-inch pockets: makes 34-36
3-inch pockets: makes 24-28

4-inch pockets: makes 20-24

CREAM CHEESE PASTRY DOUGH

This is a wonderful pastry for nut fillings.

6 oz. cream cheese, softened
1 cup butter, softened
1 tsp. grated lemon or orange peel, optional
2-2¼ cups unbleached all-purpose flour

With an electric mixer or food processor, blend cream cheese with butter. Add grated peel, if using, and flour and mix until a dough is formed. Divide dough into 3 equal portions and press each portion into a disk. Wrap each disk tightly in plastic. Refrigerate for at least 2 hours.

Preheat oven to 375°. Bake filled pockets for 15 to 20 minutes.

SUGGESTED SIZES AND YIELDS
2-inch pockets: makes 28-30   **4-inch pockets: makes 20-22**
3-inch pockets: makes 22-24

INDIAN YOGURT DOUGH

This dough recipe is based on naan, a traditional Indian flatbread. Instead of making the bread (a cross between pita and a tortilla), the dough is used as the wrapper for pockets. Bread machine owners can make the dough on the dough cycle and let the machine knead the dough for about 15 minutes. There is no need to melt the butter when using a bread machine. Use this for any Middle Eastern-flavored meat or cheese filling.

2 cups unbleached all-purpose flour
½ tsp. salt
1 tsp. sugar
1 tsp. baking powder
1 egg
¼ cup nonfat plain yogurt
¼-⅓ cup milk
2 tbs. butter, melted

In a large bowl, combine flour, salt, sugar and baking powder. In another bowl, mix together egg, yogurt, milk and melted butter. Pour liquids into flour mixture and mix well with an electric mixer or spoon until a dough is formed. Knead dough on a lightly floured work surface until smooth and elastic, about 10 minutes. Place dough in a lightly greased bowl or plastic bag and let it rest in a warm, draft-free location for about 3 hours.

Preheat oven to 400°. Bake filled pockets for about 8 to 12 minutes.

SUGGESTED SIZES AND YIELDS
3-inch pockets: makes 20-25   **6-inch pockets: makes 5-6**
4-inch pockets: makes 15-20

TORTILLA DOUGH

Using uncooked tortilla dough as the wrapper for quesadilla or other Mexican fillings allows the dough to seal tightly while still giving the tortilla flavor. Masa harina (white corn flour) is found in many large grocery stores, usually in the Mexican section, and can be called "maseca." A good stone-ground cornmeal can be substituted if masa harina is unavailable. Pockets made from this dough can be baked, or fried in deep fat for about 4 to 5 minutes, turning occasionally. Or, cook tortilla pockets on a hot, lightly greased griddle (or cast iron skillet) for about 3 minutes on each side until golden brown. This dough goes well with any spicy Mexican- or Indian curry-flavored filling.

1 cup masa harina or stone-ground cornmeal
2 cups unbleached all-purpose flour
$\frac{1}{2}$ tsp. salt
$1\frac{1}{2}$ tbs. vegetable or canola oil
$1\frac{1}{4}$-$1\frac{1}{2}$ cups warm water

In a large bowl, combine masa harina, flour and salt. Add oil and mix well. Add water, mixing until a soft dough is formed. Continue to mix or knead for about 2 minutes. Place dough in a lightly greased bowl or plastic bag and let it rest at room temperature for about 1 hour. If desired, wrap dough tightly and refrigerate for up to 24 hours before rolling.

Preheat oven to 375°. Bake filled pockets for 10 to 15 minutes.

SUGGESTED SIZES AND YIELDS

2-inch pockets: makes 44-48
3-inch pockets: makes 20-25
4-inch pockets: makes 18-24

6-inch pockets: makes 12-15
8-inch pockets: makes 10-12

EGG PASTA DOUGH

Most people are very familiar with meat or cheese ravioli. A pasta turnover is essentially the same thing. Try any of the meat or cheese fillings for a change of pace. If you have a bread machine, put the dough ingredients in the pan and let the machine knead the dough for about 5 minutes. A pasta machine can be used to roll the dough very thin — much thinner than you could get it if you rolled it by hand. Therefore, machine-rolled pasta dough yields many more pockets. Don't roll it all the way to the thinnest setting, however. The second thinnest setting works the best. When filling egg pasta pockets, it is not necessary to brush them with egg wash. If desired, you can use water to seal the dough. Depending on the filling, serve pasta pockets with tomato sauce, melted butter or olive oil and freshly grated Parmesan cheese.

2 cups semolina (pasta flour)
2 eggs
1 tbs. vegetable oil
2-4 tbs. water, optional

6-8 qt. water
salt, optional
vegetable oil, optional

Place semolina, eggs and oil in the workbowl of a food processor. Process for about 1 minute until dough starts to come together. If necessary, add water 1 tablespoon at a time until dough forms a round ball. Process for 1 to 2 additional minutes to knead dough. Divide dough into 2 or 3 balls, wrap each ball in plastic and let it rest at room temperature for about 5 minutes.

Follow instructions for rolling pastry dough on page 31. Or, roll dough with a pasta machine, according to manufacturer's instructions, to the second thinnest setting.

To cook filled pockets, bring 6 to 8 quarts water to a rapid boil. If desired, add a little salt and/or vegetable oil. Add pasta pockets to boiling water slowly, stirring to prevent sticking. Cook for 3 to 5 minutes, until done as desired. Drain well.

SUGGESTED SIZES AND YIELDS
2-inch pockets: makes 40-48 hand rolled; 55-60 machine rolled
3-inch pockets: makes 24-28 hand rolled; 34-40 machine rolled

4-inch pockets: makes 20-24 hand rolled; 28-30 machine rolled

CHINESE DUMPLING DOUGH

*Whether called pot stickers or Chinese dumplings (or gyoza in Japan), these pockets are made with a dough that is nothing more than flour and water. The secret to success is in the cooking method. Use any Asian or meat filling; the **Ginger Shrimp Filling**, page 102, is wonderful wrapped in this dough. Serve with a Chinese dipping sauce or with a little olive oil, depending on the filling.*

2 cups unbleached all-purpose flour
⅝ to ⅔ cup water

4-6 qt. water
½ cup cold water

Place flour in a bowl. Add ⅝ cup water and mix with an electric mixer or fork until blended, adding additional water if necessary. Remove from bowl and knead for about 5 minutes. Shape dough into 2 smooth balls. Wrap each ball in plastic and rest dough at room temperature for about 30 minutes.

To cook filled pockets, bring 4 to 6 quarts water to a rapid boil. Add dumplings, stirring to prevent sticking. Bring water to a second boil, add ½ cup COLD water and bring to a third boil. Cook until dumplings float to the top, about 1 minute. Remove with a slotted spoon and drain well.

SUGGESTED SIZES AND YIELDS
2-inch pockets: makes 35-40   **3-inch pockets: 25-30**

CHAPATI DOUGH

This dough is based on a recipe for an East Indian bread that is traditionally served with curry meals. Use any Middle Eastern meat or poultry filling, especially curry-flavored. Pockets made from this dough can be baked, or fried in deep fat for 4 to 5 minutes, turning occasionally. Or, cook chapati pockets on a hot, lightly greased griddle (or cast iron skillet) for about 3 minutes on each side until golden brown.

2½ cups unbleached all-purpose flour
½ cup wheat bran
½ tsp. salt

2 tbs. vegetable or canola oil
1 cup water

In a large bowl, combine flour, wheat bran and salt. In a separate bowl, mix oil with water; add to dry mixture and mix until a soft dough is formed. Continue to mix or knead for about 2 minutes. Place dough in a lightly greased bowl or plastic bag and let it rest at room temperature for about 30 to 40 minutes.

Preheat oven to 400°. Bake filled pockets for 12 to 18 minutes.

SUGGESTED SIZES AND YIELDS
3-inch pockets: makes 20-24
4-inch pockets: makes 15-20

6-inch pockets: makes 5-6

READY-MADE WRAPPERS

ABOUT READY-MADE WRAPPERS

Edible pockets can be made from many types of wrappers, including unexpected ones. Refrigerated pie crust, egg roll wrappers, biscuit dough, crescent roll dough, flour tortillas, pizza crust dough or French bread dough all make good edible pockets. Frozen doughs work well too, such as puff pastry or phyllo. You probably have many of these items on hand in the refrigerator or freezer. One limit to ready-made wrappers, however, is that they usually can't be rerolled to make more pockets from the remaining dough. See page 9 for ideas on what to do with leftover dough.

Many pockets made from ready-made wrappers can be assembled ahead of time and refrigerated or frozen for a quick dinner on a night when you're too busy to cook. Puff pastry pockets, for example, can be frozen before baking (do not use a filling containing uncooked eggs). When ready to bake, remove the pockets from the freezer and bake for 1 to 2 minutes longer than called for. Assembled phyllo pockets can be placed on a lightly buttered baking sheet, covered loosely with foil or plastic wrap and refrigerated for up to 8 hours before baking.

Some ready-made wrappers, such as egg roll wrappers and flour tortillas, are difficult to seal securely. Use extra care when pressing the sides together. A turnover press is especially helpful when using ready-made wrappers because the extra leverage and graduated teeth help to form a more secure seal.

PIE CRUST

Keeping pie crust dough on hand in the refrigerator will always enable you to throw pockets together at the last minute. Use pie crust for any filling, sweet or savory. Look for flat pie crusts in the refrigerated section of the grocery store, not the frozen crusts in pie tins in the freezer section. Keep unused pie crust in the refrigerator.

1 pkg. (16 oz.) refrigerated pie crust (makes two 9-inch pies)

Preheat oven to 400°. Remove package from the refrigerator and let dough sit unopened at room temperature for 5 to 10 minutes. Unfold 1 pie crust on a lightly floured work surface. Smooth seams and place a sheet of plastic wrap on top of dough. Follow directions on page 32 for making pastry pockets. Repeat process with remaining crust. Bake filled pockets for 12 to 18 minutes.

SUGGESTED SIZES AND YIELDS

2-inch pockets: makes 30-32	**4-inch pockets: makes 20-22**
3-inch pockets: makes 24-28	**6-inch pockets: makes 6**

PUFF PASTRY

This classic French pastry is made by folding and rolling cold dough around cold butter several times. It is somewhat complicated to make at home. Frozen puff pastry is easy to find in the freezer case in the grocery store. Any meat or cheese filling can be used. One of the easiest and most elegant appetizers you can make is to wrap small slices of Brie cheese in puff pastry. Add a little chopped fresh basil or mint if desired. Frozen puff pastry should be thawed at room temperature for 30 minutes. Thawed puff pastry can be refrigerated for up to 1 week. Do not reroll puff pastry to make extra pockets, as they will turn out too heavy.

1 pkg. (17.25 oz.) frozen puff pastry, thawed (2 sheets)

Preheat oven to 400°. Place 1 pastry sheet on a very lightly floured work surface. Follow directions for making pastry pockets on page 32. Repeat process with remaining sheet. Bake filled pockets for 12 to 20 minutes.

SUGGESTED SIZES AND YIELDS
2-inch pockets: makes 30-40
3-inch pockets: makes 14-18

4-inch pockets: makes 12-13

PHYLLO

Phyllo is readily available in the frozen section of most large grocery stores or in the dairy section in Greek or Middle Eastern markets. Almost any cheese or meat filling can be used, but I particularly like lamb, feta or other Middle Eastern-flavored fillings. For best results, thaw frozen phyllo overnight or for up to 2 days in the refrigerator. Let it sit at room temperature for about 2 hours before using. Thawed phyllo will last 2 weeks in the refrigerator if properly wrapped. The key to a flaky phyllo wrapper is to lightly brush each phyllo sheet with clarified butter. Melted butter, oil or nonstick vegetable spray can also be used.

½ cup butter   1 lb. frozen phyllo, thawed

For clarified butter, slowly melt butter in a heavy pan over low heat, frequently skimming the foam that rises to the top. Continue to heat butter and skim foam until a clear yellow liquid is visible and the white milk solids from butter sink to the bottom of pan. Carefully ladle liquid into a glass or small pitcher. Discard milk solids.

Preheat oven to 350°. Place one sheet of phyllo on a work surface and brush with clarified butter, starting at the edges and brushing toward the center. Use enough butter to lightly cover, but not to saturate, phyllo sheet. As you are working, keep remaining phyllo sheets covered with plastic wrap and a damp towel to prevent drying out. Place another sheet of phyllo directly on top of the first, and brush with butter. Repeat layering until pastry is 3 layers thick.

For 3-inch phyllo pockets, cut layered phyllo lengthwise into 4 equal strips. Place 1 to 2 tsp. filling on the lower left corner of each phyllo strip. Fold top corners over filling so that left edge is lined up with bottom edge. Continue to fold from left to right in a triangle shape until filling is completely enclosed.

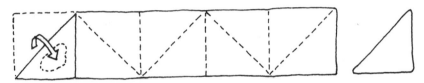

For 6-inch phyllo pockets, cut layered phyllo in half lengthwise. Place ¼ to ⅓ cup filling on the lower left corner of each phyllo strip. Continue as directed for 3-inch pockets.

Repeat layering and folding procedures until all phyllo sheets are used. Brush tops of pockets with butter. Bake filled pockets for 12 to 15 minutes, until golden brown and crisp.

SUGGESTED SIZES AND YIELDS
3-inch pockets: makes 24-32   **6-inch pockets: makes 12-16**

EGG ROLL WRAPPERS

Egg roll wrappers scream for Asian-flavored fillings, although any meat or cheese filling is equally delicious. While pockets made with egg roll wrappers can be baked, I much prefer frying them in deep fat for 2 to 3 minutes, turning occasionally. They're also delicious boiled as dumplings. Look for egg roll wrappers in the produce section of the grocery store. Each package contains about twenty 6-x-6-inch wrappers.

1 pkg. (16 oz.) egg roll wrappers
6 qt. water, optional
½ cup cold water, optional

Preheat oven to 350°. Place wrappers on a work surface. Follow directions on page 34 for making pastry pockets. Place filled pockets on a greased baking sheet. Bake for 10 to 12 minutes.

To boil filled pockets, bring 6 quarts water to a rapid boil in a large pot. Add pockets and ½ cup COLD water. After pockets rise to the surface, cook for about 45 seconds. Remove with a slotted spoon and drain well.

SUGGESTED SIZES AND YIELDS

2-inch pockets: makes 100	**4-inch pockets: makes 20**
3-inch pockets: makes 60	**6-inch pockets: makes 20**

BISCUITS

Tubes of ready-made biscuit dough, found in the dairy section of the grocery store, are marvelous tools for making pockets. Any type of biscuits can be used, and the pockets will be ready in a flash. Because this dough makes only 8 pockets, it is a great way to use up ¼ to ⅓ cup of leftovers.

1 pkg. (7½ oz.) refrigerated biscuit dough (makes 8 biscuits)

Preheat oven to 400°. Separate biscuit dough and roll or press each section as thinly as possible, about ⅛ inch. Brush with egg wash, fill with a teaspoon of desired filling and press sides closed with your fingers or a turnover press. Bake filled pockets for about 10 minutes.

SUGGESTED SIZES AND YIELDS
2½-3-inch pockets: makes 8

CRESCENT ROLLS

Refrigerated crescent roll dough offers another quick option for making pockets. Do not reroll the crescent dough, but smaller pockets can be made from the leftovers.

1 pkg. (8 oz.) refrigerated crescent rolls

Preheat oven to 375°. Unwrap package and place dough on a lightly floured counter or pastry cloth. Pinch seams closed and place a sheet of plastic wrap on top of the dough. Roll dough into a 10-x-12-inch rectangle, about ⅛-inch thick. Follow instructions for cutting and filling pastry dough pockets on page 32. Bake filled pockets for 10 to 15 minutes.

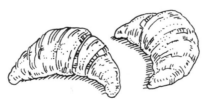

SUGGESTED SIZES AND YIELDS
3-inch pockets: makes 12   **4-inch pockets: makes 10**

FLOUR TORTILLAS

Purchased flour tortillas can be used with success. Take extra care to seal flour tortilla pockets firmly. Pockets made from flour tortillas are great when baked, but they're even better grilled like a quesadilla. If you use 10-inch tortillas, you can make twice as many 4-inch pockets, since you can cut two 4-inch circles from each tortilla.

1 pkg.(11.5 oz.) 6-inch flour tortillas (10 tortillas)

Preheat oven to 375°. Follow instructions on page 32 for cutting and filling pastry dough pockets. Seal pockets securely. Bake filled pockets for 12 to 15 minutes.

To grill filled pockets, cook on a hot, lightly greased griddle (or cast iron skillet) for about 3 minutes on each side, until golden brown.

SUGGESTED SIZES AND YIELDS
3-inch pockets: makes 30   **6-inch pockets: makes 10**
4-inch pockets: makes 10

PIZZA CRUST OR FRENCH BREAD

Although pizza crust and French bread wrappers are interchangeable when making pockets, I found pizza dough much easier to unroll than French bread dough. These doughs can be rerolled to get more pockets.

1 pkg. (10 oz.) refrigerated pizza or French bread dough

Preheat oven to 375°. Unwrap dough and place on a lightly floured work surface. Roll the dough into a 10-x-12-inch rectangle, about ⅛-inch thick. Follow instructions for cutting and filling yeast dough on page 13. Place pockets on an ungreased baking sheet and brush tops with egg wash. Bake filled pockets for 12 to 18 minutes.

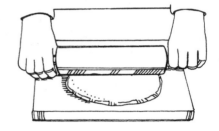

SUGGESTED SIZES AND YIELDS

3-inch pockets: makes 12-18   **4-inch pockets: makes 10-12**

SAVORY FILLINGS:
POULTRY, MEAT AND SEAFOOD

CHICKEN CURRY FILLING

Makes about 1¼ cups

There are endless variations of curry powders available in gourmet food, kitchen specialty and health food stores, as well as from mail order catalogs.

1 tsp. sesame oil
½ lb. ground chicken or turkey
¼ cup minced onion
2 cloves garlic, minced

1 tsp. grated ginger root
½-1 tsp. chopped jalapeño pepper
2 tsp.-1 tbs. curry powder
3 tbs. plain nonfat yogurt

In a large skillet, heat oil over medium heat and sauté chicken, onion and garlic until meat is no longer pink and onion is soft, about 5 to 8 minutes. Mix in ginger, jalapeño and curry and sauté for 1 to 2 minutes. Remove from heat, drain well and cool slightly. Mix in yogurt just before filling pockets.

SUGGESTED WRAPPERS:
Garlic Yeast Dough, page 23
Indian Yogurt Dough, page 42
Chapati Dough, page 49

Pie Crust, page 52
Egg Roll Wrappers, page 56

MOROCCAN CHICKEN FILLING

This recipe is based on a traditional recipe for b'steeya, a Moroccan pie made of shredded chicken, almonds, cinnamon and phyllo. For authentic flavor, add 2 tbs. slivered almonds to the filling and sprinkle baked pockets with confectioners' sugar.

½ lb. ground chicken or turkey
2 tbs. minced onion
olive oil, optional
¼ tsp. salt
½ tsp. coarsely ground pepper

½ tsp. grated ginger root
½ tsp. cinnamon
2 tbs. chopped fresh parsley, or 2 tsp. dried, crushed

In a large skillet over medium heat, sauté chicken and onion until meat is no longer pink and onion is soft, about 5 to 8 minutes. Use a small amount of olive oil if desired. Remove from heat, drain well and cool slightly. Add remaining ingredients and mix until well blended.

SUGGESTED WRAPPERS:
Orange Ginger Yeast Dough, page 29
Basic Savory Pastry Dough, page 36
Cream Cheese Pastry Dough, page 41
Chapati Dough, page 49

Pie Crust, page 52
Puff Pastry, page 53
Phyllo, page 54

GREEK CHICKEN FILLING

Makes about 1½ cups

This recipe is adapted from a traditional Greek recipe for chicken triangles (ko-topetes). It calls for boiling a chicken, removing the meat and chopping it. I use ground chicken for ease. The yogurt provides extra moisture without adding extra fat.

1 tbs. olive oil
1 tbs. chopped walnuts or pine nuts
½ lb. ground chicken
¼ cup minced onion
1 clove garlic, minced

½ cup freshly grated Parmesan cheese
¼ tsp. salt
½ tsp. coarsely ground pepper
3 tbs. plain nonfat yogurt

In a large skillet, heat oil over medium heat and sauté nuts for 2 to 3 minutes, stirring frequently. Remove nuts from pan and cool. In the same skillet, sauté ground chicken, onion and garlic until meat is no longer pink and onion is soft, about 5 to 8 minutes. Remove from heat, drain well and cool slightly. Add remaining ingredients, including nuts, and mix until well blended.

SUGGESTED WRAPPERS:
Parmesan Pepper Yeast Dough, page 27
Spinach Yeast Dough, page 28
Basic Savory Pastry Dough, page 36

Indian Yogurt Dough, page 42
Pie Crust, page 52
Pizza Crust, page 60

CUBAN CHICKEN FILLING

The combination of flavors in this filling makes for wonderful fare. In Cuba, baked or fried empanadas made with pastry or yeast doughs are a staple. A common savory filling consists of shredded chicken, tomatoes, nuts and ham or bacon. This adaptation uses ground chicken instead of cooked, shredded chicken for ease.

2 medium-sized plum tomatoes
1½ tsp. olive oil, or more if needed
2 tbs. slivered almonds
½ lb. ground chicken or turkey
3 slices (about 2 oz.) bacon, cut into ½-inch pieces
2 tbs. minced onion
1 tbs. sherry
¼ tsp. salt
½ tsp. coarsely ground pepper
¼ cup grated Swiss cheese

With a sharp knife, remove the top portion of each tomato and squeeze out seeds and juice. Coarsely chop tomatoes and drain any excess juice; set aside. In a large skillet, heat oil over medium-high heat and and sauté almonds for 2 to 3 minutes, stirring frequently. Remove nuts from pan and cool. In the same skillet over medium heat, sauté chicken, bacon and onion until chicken is no longer pink and onion is soft, about 5 to 8 minutes. Use a small amount of olive oil if desired. Add diced tomatoes, sherry, salt and pepper and sauté for 1 to 2 minutes. Remove from heat, drain well and cool slightly. Add cheese and sautéed nuts and mix until well blended.

SUGGESTED WRAPPERS:
Whole Wheat Yeast Dough, page 20   *Pie Crust*, page 52
Onion Yeast Dough, page 25   *Puff Pastry*, page 53
Basic Savory Pastry Dough, page 36

TURKISH CHICKEN PIE FILLING

Makes about 1½ cups

This filling is adapted from a recipe for Turkish boreks that uses cooked chicken wrapped in phyllo. The special combination of herbs and spices is commonly found in Turkish cuisine. If desired, add about 2 tbs. toasted chopped pistachio nuts for crunch.

2 medium-sized plum tomatoes
½ lb. ground chicken or turkey
2 tbs. minced onion
1 clove garlic, minced
olive oil, optional
½ tsp. ground thyme
¼ tsp. salt
½ tsp. coarsely ground pepper
3 tbs. chopped fresh parsley, or 1 tbs. dried, crushed
1 tbs. chopped fresh basil, or 1 tsp. dried, crushed

With a sharp knife, remove the top portion of each tomato and squeeze out seeds and juice. Coarsely chop tomatoes and drain any excess juice; set aside. In a large skillet over medium heat, sauté chicken, onion and garlic until meat is no longer pink and onion is soft, about 5 to 8 minutes. Use a small amount olive oil if desired. Add diced tomatoes and remaining ingredients and sauté for 1 to 2 minutes. Remove from heat, drain well and cool slightly.

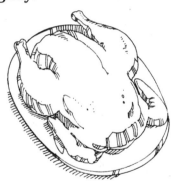

SUGGESTED WRAPPERS:
Garlic Herb Yeast Dough
  with basil or parsley, page 24
Indian Yogurt Dough, **page 42**

Chapati Dough, **page 49**
Pie Crust, **page 52**
Phyllo, **page 54**

SPICY ASIAN CHICKEN FILLING

This filling calls for several traditional Asian ingredients that are easily found in any large grocery store. Sesame oil can be found either in the Asian foods section or with the cooking oils. Fresh cilantro, the leaves of the coriander plant, is found with the fresh herbs in the produce section of the grocery store. It may be called "Chinese parsley" or "fresh coriander." It looks like Italian parsley, but has a very distinctive aroma and flavor.

1 tbs. sesame oil
½ lb. ground chicken or turkey
1 clove garlic, minced
1 tbs. hoisin sauce
1 tbs. soy sauce
1 tsp. grated ginger root
¼ tsp. salt
½ tsp. crushed red pepper flakes
¼ cup chopped fresh cilantro

In a large skillet, heat oil over medium heat and sauté chicken with garlic, hoisin sauce, soy sauce, ginger root, salt and pepper until meat is no longer pink, about 5 to 8 minutes. Add cilantro and sauté for 1 to 2 minutes. Remove from heat, drain well and cool slightly.

SUGGESTED WRAPPERS:
Garlic Yeast Dough, page 23
Chinese Dumpling Dough, page 48
Chapati Dough, page 49

Pie Crust, page 52
Egg Roll Wrappers, page 56

ITALIAN HAM FILLING

Makes about 1½ cups

You can double this recipe, but keep the ratios the same. Sliced meat and cheese can be used, but I find diced or grated ingredients easier to eat in a pocket. Use prosciutto, capricola or another variety of Italian ham. You can also use a salt-cured domestic country ham.

½ cup diced Italian ham
½ cup diced hard or Genoa salami
¼ cup grated provolone cheese
¼ cup grated mozzarella cheese
½ tsp. coarsely ground pepper

Mix all ingredients until well blended.

SUGGESTED WRAPPERS:
Rye Yeast Dough, page 19
Tomato Basil Yeast Dough, page 22
Parmesan Pepper Yeast Dough, page 27
Spinach Yeast Dough, page 28

Basic Savory Pastry Dough, page 36
Indian Yogurt Dough, page 42
Pie Crust, page 52
Pizza Crust, page 60

ITALIAN HAM AND SPINACH FILLING

Makes about 2 cups

This flavorful filling combines vegetables, protein and dairy. Enclosed in a dough wrapper, it makes a true meal in one. If desired, you can substitute a salt-cured domestic country ham for the prosciutto.

1 pkg. (10 oz.) frozen chopped spinach, thawed
1 tbs. olive oil
1 clove garlic, minced

½ cup diced Italian ham or salami
¼ cup grated mozzarella cheese
½ tsp. coarsely ground pepper

Drain spinach well and squeeze dry. In a large skillet, heat oil over medium-high heat and sauté spinach and garlic until spinach is just tender, about 3 minutes. Remove from heat, drain well and cool slightly. Add remaining ingredients and mix until well blended.

SUGGESTED WRAPPERS:
Lemon Mint Yeast Dough, page 26
Parmesan Pepper Yeast Dough, page 27
Indian Yogurt Dough, page 42
Egg Pasta Dough, page 46

Chapati Dough, page 49
Pie Crust, page 52
Puff Pastry, page 53
Pizza Crust, page 60

SPANISH HAM FILLING

In Spain, small dishes or "tapas" are an important part of the cuisine. This filling is based on a tapas recipe for savory turnovers. The use of hard-cooked eggs in recipes is common in Spain, the Caribbean and South America. Use any good deli ham, and, if desired, place a small piece of cheese on top of the filling before sealing. I use provolone, but just about any cheese could be used.

2 medium-sized plum tomatoes
1 cup diced ham
2 tbs. minced onion

2 hard-cooked eggs, quartered
¼ tsp. salt
¼ tsp. coarsely ground pepper

With a sharp knife, remove the top portion of each tomato and squeeze out seeds and juice. Chop tomatoes coarsely and drain any excess juice. Combine all ingredients in the workbowl of a food processor and process until mixture is finely minced and well blended.

SUGGESTED WRAPPERS:
Rye Yeast Dough, page 19
Garlic Yeast Dough, page 23
Onion Yeast Dough, page 25
Basic Savory Pastry Dough, page 36

Vienna Pastry Dough, page 40
Pie Crust, page 52
Puff Pastry, page 53
Crescent Rolls, page 58

ASIAN PORK FILLING

Makes about 1½ cups

This is a very simple and flavorful meat filling. Wrap it with egg roll wrappers and serve as an appetizer. Wrap it in yeast dough and serve as a light meal with an Asian-flavored salad. Sesame oil, soy sauce, and ginger root are common ingredients used in Asian cooking. Look for the ingredients in the Asian foods section of the grocery store.

½ lb. ground pork
1 tbs. sesame oil
2 tbs. soy sauce
1 tsp. grated ginger root
¼ tsp. salt
½ tsp. dry mustard, regular or hot

Mix all ingredients until well blended. In a large skillet over medium heat, sauté mixture until meat is no longer pink, about 5 to 8 minutes. Remove from heat, drain well and cool slightly.

SUGGESTED WRAPPERS:
Orange Ginger Yeast Dough, page 29
Indian Yogurt Dough, page 42

Chinese Dumpling Dough, page 48
Egg Roll Wrappers, page 56

SAUSAGE EGGPLANT FILLING

This filling is a little more elaborate than some of the others, but it's worth the time and effort it takes to make it. Make 6- or 8-inch pockets for a light meal with a salad. Try to use small eggplants as they are more tender. Use bulk sausage, or remove links from their casings so that it can be easily crumbled. A small piece of provolone cheese can be placed on top of the filling just before sealing if desired.

2 medium-sized plum tomatoes
1/2 lb. eggplant
1/2 tsp. salt
1/2 lb. Italian sausage
1 tbs. olive oil
1/4 cup minced onion
1/2 tsp. coarsely ground pepper
1/2 tsp. minced jalapeño pepper, or to taste, optional
1 tbs. chopped fresh parsley
1 tbs. chopped fresh cilantro

With a sharp knife, remove the top portion of each tomato and squeeze out seeds and juice. Coarsely chop tomatoes and drain any excess juice; set aside. With a sharp knife, remove the top portion of eggplant. Chop coarsely, sprinkle with salt and toss to coat well. Place in a colander and drain for 20 to 30 minutes. Squeeze dry.

In a large skillet over medium-high heat, sauté sausage until no longer pink, about 5 to 8 minutes; drain well, crumble and set aside. In the same skillet, heat oil over medium heat and sauté onion until golden, about 2 to 3 minutes. Add eggplant and sauté until eggplant is just tender, about 5 minutes. Add tomatoes, sausage and remaining ingredients and sauté for 1 to 2 minutes, until tomatoes are soft. Remove from heat, drain well and cool slightly.

SUGGESTED WRAPPERS:
Garlic Yeast Dough, page 23   *Tortilla Dough*, page 44
Onion Yeast Dough, page 25   *Pizza Crust*, page 60

BACON AND CHEESE FILLING

Makes about 3 cups

Dice the tomato instead of slicing it if you are making small, appetizer-sized turnovers. Use crumbled feta cheese instead of Parmesan for an exciting variation.

1 lb. sliced bacon
½ cup ricotta cheese
1 egg yolk
¼ cup freshly grated Parmesan cheese
2 medium-sized plum tomatoes

In a large skillet over medium-high heat, cook bacon until crisp; drain well, crumble and set aside. In a bowl, blend ricotta cheese with egg yolk. Add Parmesan and crumbled bacon and mix until just blended. With a sharp knife, remove the top portion of each tomato and squeeze out seeds and juice. Slice tomatoes thinly and drain any excess juice. Fill pocket with bacon and cheese mixture and top with a single tomato slice before sealing.

SUGGESTED WRAPPERS:
Parmesan Pepper Yeast Dough, page 27   **Pie Crust, page 52**
Basic Savory Pastry Dough, page 36   **Phyllo, page 54**

MEAT CALZONE FILLING

Makes about 2 cups

Use whatever meat is preferred in your house. If you want to get fancy, place a small amount of your favorite pizza topping on top of the meat before sealing the pockets. A slice or two of mushroom, a few pieces of diced green pepper or a couple of onion slices work well. Be careful not to overfill, though.

½ lb. ground beef or bulk Italian sausage
½ cup pizza sauce
1 cup (4 oz.) grated mozzarella cheese

In a large skillet over medium heat, sauté beef until no longer pink, about 5 to 8 minutes. Remove from heat, drain well and crumble. Add remaining ingredients and mix until well blended.

SUGGESTED WRAPPERS:
Rye Yeast Dough, page 19
Tomato Basil Yeast Dough, page 22
Parmesan Pepper Yeast Dough, page 27
Spinach Yeast Dough, page 28

Basic Savory Pastry Dough, page 36
Indian Yogurt Dough, page 42
Pie Crust, page 52
Pizza Crust, page 60

TACO FILLING

Pockets made from this filling make great lunches for kids of all ages. I like using ground turkey for a low-fat alternative. My husband and I prefer to use salsa, but the kids prefer sour cream. I usually make some of each. Use cheddar, Monterey Jack or a combination of cheeses.

1/2 lb. ground beef or turkey
1/2 pkg. (1 1/4 oz. pkg.) taco seasoning
1 cup (4 oz.) grated cheese
1/4 cup salsa or sour cream

Cook meat according to directions on taco seasoning packet, adding water if called for. While meat is still warm, add remaining ingredients and mix until well blended. Cool slightly.

SUGGESTED WRAPPERS:
Mexican Yeast Dough, page 21
Tortilla Dough, page 44

Pie Crust, page 52
Flour Tortillas, page 59

MEAT PIROSHKI FILLING

Makes about 2 cups

Pockets made from this Russian filling can be eaten for lunch or dinner. The cabbage adds a wonderful flavor. The traditional wrapper for piroshki is a paper-thin pastry dough, but I enjoy using yeast wrappers for a light meal.

½ lb. ground beef or turkey	2 tbs. whipping cream
2 tbs. minced onion	1 tsp. caraway seeds
1 clove garlic, minced	1 tsp. dill weed
1 cup shredded green cabbage	¼ tsp. salt
1 large potato, cooked and grated	½ tsp. coarsely ground pepper

In a large skillet over medium heat, sauté beef, onion and garlic until meat is no longer pink and onion is soft, about 5 to 8 minutes. Add cabbage and sauté for about 10 minutes, stirring frequently. Remove from heat, drain well and cool slightly. Add remaining ingredients and mix until well blended.

SUGGESTED WRAPPERS:
Garlic Herb Yeast Dough with dill, page 24
Basic Savory Pastry Dough, page 36
Tortilla Dough, page 44

Pie Crust, page 52
Phyllo, page 54

SAVORY FILLINGS: POULTRY, MEAT AND SEAFOOD   81

MEXICAN EMPANADA FILLING

This recipe uses many foods that are native to the Americas, including potatoes, tomatoes, and, if you wrap the filling in tortillas, corn. If you cannot find pine nuts, or prefer a less expensive alternative, use chopped walnuts.

2 medium-sized plum tomatoes
1 tbs. vegetable oil
2 tbs. chopped pine nuts
½ lb. ground beef
1 small potato, very finely diced
¼ cup minced onion
1 clove garlic, minced
¼ tsp. salt
½ tsp. coarsely ground pepper
2 tbs. chopped fresh cilantro, or 2 tsp. dried, crushed
2 tbs. raisins

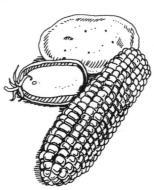

With a sharp knife, remove the top portion of each tomato and squeeze out seeds and juice. Coarsely chop tomatoes and drain any excess juice; set aside. In a large skillet, heat ½ tbs. of the oil over medium-high heat and sauté nuts for 2 to 3 minutes, stirring frequently. Remove nuts from pan and cool. In the same skillet, heat remaining oil over medium heat and sauté beef, potato, onion and garlic until meat is no longer pink and onion is soft, about 5 to 8 minutes; drain well. Add salt, pepper, cilantro and tomatoes and sauté for 1 to 2 minutes. Remove from heat and cool slightly. Mix in raisins and nuts.

SUGGESTED WRAPPERS:
Garlic Herb Yeast Dough,
   with cilantro, page 24
Onion Yeast Dough, page 25
Cream Cheese Pastry Dough, page 41

Tortilla Dough, page 44
Chapati Dough, page 49
Pie Crust, page 52
Flour Tortillas, page 59

SOUTH AMERICAN EMPANADA FILLING

Makes about 1½ cups

Using raisins in meat fillings is popular throughout South America and the Caribbean. In Chile, these traditional meat pies are enjoyed as late-afternoon snacks, often purchased from street vendors.

2 tbs. raisins
2 tbs. sherry
½ tbs. butter or margarine
2 tbs. chopped walnuts or sliced almonds, optional
½ lb. ground beef
¼ cup minced onion
¼ tsp. salt
½ tsp. coarsely ground pepper
2 tbs. chopped fresh parsley, or 2 tsp. dried, crushed

In a small bowl, mix raisins with sherry; set aside. In a large skillet, heat butter over medium-high heat and sauté nuts for 2 to 3 minutes, stirring frequently. Remove nuts from pan and cool.

In the same skillet over medium heat, sauté beef and onion until meat is no longer pink and onion is soft, about 5 to 8 minutes; drain well. Stir in salt, pepper and parsley and sauté for 1 to 2 minutes. Remove from heat, drain well and cool slightly. Add nuts and soaked raisins and mix until well blended.

SUGGESTED WRAPPERS:
Garlic Herb Yeast Dough with parsley, page 24   *Chapati Dough*, page 49
Onion Yeast Dough, page 25   *Pie Crust*, page 52
Cream Cheese Pastry Dough, page 41   *Flour Tortillas*, page 59

VARIATION: CHILEAN EMPANADA FILLING

Omit walnuts. Add 2 tsp. paprika and $\frac{1}{2}$ tsp. ground cumin with the salt and pepper. Sprinkle 1 can (4.25 oz.) drained sliced black olives and 2 chopped hard-cooked eggs over meat mixture before sealing pockets.

SUGGESTED WRAPPERS:
Garlic Herb Yeast Dough with parsley, page 24   *Chapati Dough*, page 49
Indian Yogurt Dough, page 42   *Pie Crust*, page 52
Tortilla Dough, page 44   *Flour Tortillas*, page 59

INTERNATIONAL MEAT PIE FILLING

Cinnamon is used to flavor meat all over the world. If desired, allspice can be used as a substitute and either spice can be adjusted to taste. Use walnuts, pine nuts or pistachio nuts. Ground turkey or lamb can be substituted for ground beef.

1½ tsp. olive or vegetable oil
2 tbs. chopped nuts
½ lb. ground beef
¼ cup minced onion
1 clove garlic, minced
¼ tsp. salt
½ tsp. coarsely ground pepper
¼ tsp. cinnamon
2 tbs. chopped fresh parsley, or 2 tsp. dried, crushed

In a large skillet, heat oil over medium-high heat and sauté nuts for 2 to 3 minutes, stirring frequently. Remove nuts from pan and cool. In the same skillet, sauté beef and onion until meat is no longer pink and onion is soft, about 5 to 8 minutes. Stir in remaining ingredients, except nuts. Remove from heat, drain well and cool slightly. Add nuts and mix until well blended.

SUGGESTED WRAPPERS:
Garlic Herb Yeast Dough
　with parsley, page 24
Onion Yeast Dough, **page 25**

Tortilla Dough, **page 44**
Chapati Dough, **page 49**
Pie Crust, **page 52**

AFGHANISTANI MEAT PIE FILLING

Makes about 1½ cups

This filling is based on a traditional Afghanistani recipe for Sambosay Goshti, which is wrapped in a pastry dough and deep-fat fried. If you have garam masala, a potent spice blend, use about ½ to ¾ tsp. in place of the spices. You'll still need to use salt and pepper, however. You can adjust any of the spices to taste.

½ lb. ground beef	¼ tsp. cinnamon
¼ cup minced onion	¼ tsp. ground cardamom
1 clove garlic, minced	⅛ tsp. ground cumin
olive oil, optional	⅛ tsp. ground coriander
⅛ tsp. salt	pinch ground cloves
½ tsp. coarsely ground pepper	pinch ground mace

In a large skillet over medium heat, sauté ground beef, onion and garlic until meat is no longer pink and onion is soft, about 5 to 8 minutes. Use a small amount of olive oil if desired. Add remaining ingredients and sauté for 1 to 2 minutes. Remove from heat, drain well and cool slightly.

SUGGESTED WRAPPERS:
Garlic Yeast Dough, page 23
Tortilla Dough, page 44
Chapati Dough, page 49

Pie Crust, page 52
Puff Pastry, page 53

PAKISTANI MEAT PIE FILLING

Makes about 1½ cups

This filling is loosely based on a Pakistani meatball and curry dish, served to us by a Pakistani family in Monterey, California. It's a winner with both beef and lamb. Fresh cilantro has the best flavor for this recipe, and is easy to find in the produce section of the supermarket. I strongly recommend using it over dried cilantro.

½ lb. ground beef or lamb
¼ cup minced onion
1 clove garlic, minced
½ tsp. grated ginger root
½ tsp. ground cumin
½ tsp. ground coriander

¼ tsp. turmeric
¼ tsp. salt
½ tsp. coarsely ground pepper
1 tbs. chopped fresh cilantro, or 1 tsp. dried, crushed

In a large skillet over medium heat, sauté beef, onion and garlic until meat is no longer pink and onion is soft, about 5 to 8 minutes. Add remaining ingredients and mix until well blended. Remove from heat, drain well and cool slightly.

SUGGESTED WRAPPERS:
Garlic Herb Yeast Dough
  with cilantro, page 24
Indian Yogurt Dough, page 42

Chapati Dough, page 49
Pie Crust, page 52
Flour Tortillas, page 59

TURKISH MEAT PIE FILLING

This recipe is based on a version of Turkish boreks. The seasonings in this strongly flavored meat filling can be adjusted to taste.

1½ tsp. olive or vegetable oil
¼ cup chopped walnuts or
  pistachio nuts
½ lb. ground beef
¼ cup minced onion
1 tbs. red wine vinegar
½ tsp. salt

½ tsp. ground allspice
¼ tsp. dill weed
½ tsp. crushed red pepper flakes
½ tsp. coarsely ground pepper
2 tbs. chopped fresh parsley, or
  2 tsp. dried, crushed

In a large skillet, heat oil over medium-high heat and sauté nuts for 2 to 3 minutes, stirring frequently. Remove nuts from pan and cool. In the same skillet over medium heat, sauté beef and onion until meat is no longer pink and onion is soft, about 5 to 8 minutes. Add remaining ingredients, except nuts, and mix until well blended. Remove from heat, drain well and cool slightly. Add nuts and mix until well blended.

SUGGESTED WRAPPERS:
Garlic Herb Yeast Dough with dill, page 24
Indian Yogurt Dough, page 42
Tortilla Dough, page 44
Chapati Dough, page 49
Pie Crust, page 52

CORNISH PASTY FILLING

Makes about 1½ cups

Miners in Cornwall, England, would lunch on pastries that were filled with a combination of meat and vegetables. It provided a well-balanced meal in one. Sometimes a sweet fruit filling was placed at one end of the dough so that dessert was included. The filling is best if made a day in advance.

1 tbs. vegetable oil
¼ cup chopped onion
8 oz. chuck steak, cut into small cubes
½ cup water
½ tsp. beef bouillon granules

½ tsp. salt
½ tsp. coarsely ground pepper
2 small carrots, finely diced
1 medium potato, finely diced
¼ cup fresh or frozen peas

In a large skillet, heat oil over medium heat and sauté onion until golden and soft, about 3 to 5 minutes. With a slotted spoon, remove onion and set aside. In the same skillet, sauté beef cubes over medium-high heat until browned on all sides. Drain well. Add water, bouillon, salt, pepper, carrots, potato and onion. Reduce heat, cover and simmer for about 1 hour, stirring occasionally, until liquid has evaporated. Add peas and cook for 2 to 3 minutes. Remove from heat and cool completely.

SUGGESTED WRAPPERS:
Garlic Herb Yeast Dough with parsley, page 24
Onion Yeast Dough, page 25
Cream Cheese Pastry Dough, page 41
Pie Crust, page 52

CHINESE ORANGE BEEF FILLING

Makes about 1½ cups

I keep a very small can of frozen orange juice concentrate in the freezer just for cooking. This recipe combines many traditional Chinese ingredients.

½ lb. ground beef
1 tbs. frozen orange juice concentrate
1 tbs. soy sauce
1 tsp. sesame oil
1 tsp. rice vinegar
1 tsp. brown sugar

1 clove garlic, minced
½ tsp. grated ginger root
½ tsp. grated orange peel
¼ tsp. salt
¼ tsp. cayenne pepper

Mix all ingredients until well blended. In a large skillet over medium heat, sauté mixture until meat is no longer pink, about 5 to 8 minutes. Remove from heat, drain well and cool slightly.

SUGGESTED WRAPPERS:
***Orange Ginger Yeast Dough*, page 29**
***Indian Yogurt Dough*, page 42**

***Chinese Dumpling Dough*, page 48**
***Egg Roll Wrappers*, page 56**

INDIAN MEAT FILLING

Makes about 1½ cups

In India, meat-filled breads are typically served with yogurt. If you're serving pockets as a light meal, serve them with a yogurt dipping sauce. Or, serve them with a salad that has a yogurt-based dressing.

1 tbs. butter
½ lb. ground beef
¼ cup minced onion
¼ tsp. salt
¼-½ tsp. crushed red pepper flakes

1 tbs. chopped fresh mint, or 1 tsp. dried, crushed
1 tbs. chopped fresh cilantro, or 1 tsp. dried, crushed

In a large skillet, heat butter over medium heat and sauté ground beef and onion until meat is longer pink and onion is soft, about 5 to 8 minutes. Add remaining ingredients and sauté for 1 to 2 minutes. Remove from heat, drain well and cool slightly.

SUGGESTED WRAPPERS:
Garlic Yeast Dough, page 23
Chinese Dumpling Dough, page 48
Chapati Dough, page 49

Pie Crust, page 52
Egg Roll Wrappers, page 56

LEBANESE MEAT FILLING

This recipe calls for ingredients used in many Middle Eastern countries, such as Lebanon. Lamb is the traditional choice in this recipe, but beef works well, too. Rice is commonly used to stretch meat fillings and serves as a moistening binder. Use pine nuts, walnuts or pistachio nuts. Substitute thyme for mint if desired.

1 tbs. butter
¼ cup chopped nuts
½ lb. ground lamb or beef
¼ cup minced onion
1 clove garlic, minced
¼ tsp. salt
½ tsp. coarsely ground pepper
¼ tsp. cinnamon
1 tbs. chopped fresh parsley, or 1 tsp. dried, crushed
1 tbs. chopped fresh mint, or 1 tsp. dried, crushed
½ cup cooked rice, optional

In a large skillet, heat butter over medium-high heat and sauté nuts for 2 to 3 minutes, stirring frequently. Remove nuts from pan and cool. In the same skillet over medium heat, sauté meat, onion and garlic until meat is no longer pink and onion is soft, about 5 to 8 minutes. Drain well. Add remaining ingredients and sauté for 2 to 3 minutes. Cool slightly.

SUGGESTED WRAPPERS:
Garlic Herb Yeast Dough, **page 24**
Basic Savory Pastry Dough, **page 36**
Indian Yogurt Dough, **page 42**

Chapati Dough, **page 49**
Pie Crust, **page 52**

MIDDLE EASTERN LAMB AND FETA FILLING

This is one of my all-time favorite combinations and uses traditional Middle Eastern ingredients. This filling is also good without the cheese.

½ lb. ground lamb
¼ cup minced onion
1 clove garlic, minced
¼ tsp. salt
½ tsp. coarsely ground pepper
½ cup ricotta cheese

¼ cup (1 oz.) crumbled feta cheese
1 tbs. chopped fresh parsley, or 1 tsp.
   dried, crushed
1 tbs. chopped fresh mint, or 1 tsp.
   dried, crushed

In a large skillet over medium heat, sauté lamb, onion and garlic until meat is no longer pink and onion is soft, about 5 to 8 minutes. Drain well. Add remaining ingredients and mix until well blended. Cool slightly.

SUGGESTED WRAPPERS:
Garlic Herb Yeast Dough
  with parsley or mint, page 24
Basic Savory Pastry Dough
  with pepper, page 36

***Indian Yogurt Dough*, page 42**
***Chapati Dough*, page 49**
***Pie Crust*, page 52**

LUMPIA FILLING

Lumpia is the Philippine version of an egg roll. Instead of wrapping this filling in a traditional egg roll form, make turnovers.

1 tbs. sesame oil	4-6 water chestnuts
½ lb. ground pork	¼ cup shredded carrots or turnips
2 tbs. minced onion	1 tbs. soy sauce
1 clove garlic, minced	1 tsp. sugar
½ tsp. grated ginger root	¼ tsp. salt
¼ lb. cooked shrimp, peeled, deveined	¼-½ tsp. coarsely ground pepper

In a large skillet, heat sesame oil over medium heat and sauté pork, onion and garlic until meat is no longer pink and onion is soft, about 5 to 8 minutes. Remove from heat, drain well and cool slightly. Combine with remaining ingredients in the workbowl of a food processor. Process until finely chopped and well blended.

SUGGESTED WRAPPERS:
Garlic Yeast Dough, page 23
Orange Ginger Yeast Dough, page 29
Tortilla Dough, page 44

Chinese Dumpling Dough, page 48
Chapati Dough, page 49
Egg Roll Wrappers, page 56

TUNA AND CHEESE FILLING

Makes about 1½ cups

This filling calls for just enough mayonnaise to bind the filling together while keeping it as dietetic as possible. If you prefer, use cheddar cheese instead of American.

1 can (12 oz.) water-packed tuna, drained
3 tbs. mayonnaise
1 tbs. minced onion
1 stalk celery, finely chopped
⅛ tsp. salt
¼ tsp. coarsely ground pepper
sliced American cheese

Combine tuna with mayonnaise, onion, celery, salt and pepper and mix until well blended. Place a slice of cheese on top of tuna mixture before sealing pockets, cutting cheese to fit pockets as necessary.

SUGGESTED WRAPPERS:
Garlic Yeast Dough, page 23
Onion Yeast Dough, page 25
Indian Yogurt Dough, page 42
Chapati Dough, page 49

Pie Crust, page 52
Egg Roll Wrappers, page 56
Flour Tortillas, page 59

CRAB AND CREAM CHEESE FILLING

Makes about 1¼ cups

This filling is based on a favored crab dip. It makes superb 3-inch appetizer pockets wrapped in puff pastry. Leftover filling, if any, can be enjoyed with crackers.

6-8 oz. crabmeat
4 oz. cream cheese, softened
1 scallion, chopped
1 clove garlic, minced
1 tbs. lemon juice
2-3 drops Tabasco Sauce
¼ tsp. salt
¼-½ tsp. coarsely ground pepper
1 tbs. chopped fresh parsley, or 1 tsp. dried, crushed

Process all ingredients with a food processor until well blended.

SUGGESTED WRAPPERS:
Lemon Mint Yeast Dough
    with parsley instead of mint, page 26
Basic Savory Pastry Dough, **page 36**

Basic Sweet Pastry Dough, **page 37**
Pie Crust, **page 52**
Puff Pastry, **page 53**

CRAB AND CHEDDAR FILLING

Makes about 1½ cups

This delightful, very simple crab filling is easily increased or decreased to match the amount of crabmeat you have on hand.

6-8 oz. crabmeat
½ cup grated sharp cheddar cheese
1 scallion, chopped
4-6 drops Tabasco Sauce
¼ cup slivered or chopped almonds

Process all ingredients with a food processor until well blended.

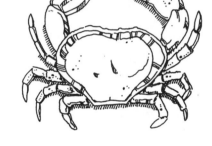

SUGGESTED WRAPPERS:
Lemon Mint Yeast Dough, page 26
Basic Savory Pastry Dough, page 36
Basic Sweet Pastry Dough, page 37

Coconut Ginger Pastry Dough, page 38
Pie Crust, page 52
Puff Pastry, page 53

SHRIMP FILLING

If using uncooked shrimp, clean it and sauté it with the onion and garlic. I usually have the seafood department of the supermarket steam the shrimp for me — some upscale grocery store chains even clean and devein it, too.

2 medium-sized plum tomatoes
1 tbs. olive oil
1/4 cup minced onion
1 clove garlic, minced
1/2 lb. cooked shrimp, peeled, deveined, cut in half

1/4 tsp. salt
1/4-1/2 tsp. coarsely ground pepper
2 tbs. chopped fresh parsley, or
   2 tsp. dried, crushed
1 hard-cooked egg, quartered

With a sharp knife, remove the top portion of each tomato and squeeze out seeds and juice. Coarsely chop tomatoes and drain any excess juice. In a large skillet, heat oil over medium-high heat and sauté onion, garlic and tomatoes until onion is golden and tomatoes are soft, about 3 to 4 minutes. Cool slightly. Place all ingredients in the workbowl of a food processor and process until coarsely chopped and well blended.

SUGGESTED WRAPPERS:
Garlic Yeast Dough, page 23
Onion Yeast Dough, page 25
Coconut Ginger Pastry Dough, page 38

Pie Crust, page 52
Flour Tortillas, page 59

GINGER SHRIMP FILLING

Makes about 1½ cups

*If you like ginger, you'll love this. **Coconut Ginger Pastry Dough**, page 38, is a sure winner with this filling. If you purchase uncooked shrimp, sauté it lightly with a little olive oil and the garlic.*

½ lb. cooked shrimp, peeled, deveined
1 clove garlic, minced
1 tbs. grated ginger root
1 scallion, green part only, chopped
½ tsp. crushed red pepper flakes
1 tsp. grated orange or lemon peel
¼ cup sweetened flaked coconut

Process all ingredients with a food processor until coarsely chopped and well blended.

SUGGESTED WRAPPERS:
Orange Ginger Yeast Dough, page 29
Coconut Ginger Pastry Dough, page 38

Pie Crust, page 52
Puff Pastry, page 53

102   SAVORY FILLINGS: POULTRY, MEAT AND SEAFOOD

SAVORY FILLINGS:
CHEESE, VEGETABLE AND HERB

ONION HERB FILLING

Makes about 1½ cups

Instead of mixing the ingredients together, I find it easier to fill the dough with the onion and sprinkle the seasonings on the top. Use mint, parsley or basil.

olive oil
1 large Bermuda or other mild onion, diced
coarse sea or Kosher salt to taste
coarsely ground pepper to taste
¼ cup chopped fresh herbs

Brush wrapper with olive oil instead of egg wash. Fill pockets with onion and sprinkle with seasonings and herbs.

SUGGESTED WRAPPERS:
Lemon Mint Yeast Dough, **page 26**
Parmesan Pepper Yeast Dough, **page 27**
Basic Savory Pastry Dough, **page 36**

Flour Tortillas, **page 59**
Pizza Crust, **page 60**

HERBED FETA FILLING

Use chopped fresh parsley, basil, dill or mint. Dried herbs don't seem to blend with the cheese very well. White pepper blends into the cheese mixture nicely. If you don't have any, black pepper can be used. Goat cheese can be substituted for feta if desired.

1 cup (4 oz.) crumbled feta cheese
1 egg yolk
¼ cup chopped fresh herbs
¼-½ tsp. white pepper

In a bowl, blend cheese with egg yolk. Stir in herbs and pepper and mix until well blended.

VARIATION: HERBED MOZZARELLA FILLING

Substitute 1½ cups grated mozzarella cheese for feta.

SUGGESTED WRAPPERS:
Garlic Herb Yeast Dough, page 24
Egg Pasta Dough, page 46

Pie Crust, page 52
Phyllo, page 54

HERBED FETA AND WALNUT FILLING

Makes about 1 cup

Use chopped fresh parsley, basil, dill or mint. Dried herbs just don't seem to blend with this. Choose herbs that complement the dough you're using. For example, mint is a good choice when using **Spinach Yeast Dough**, *page 28, or* **Lemon Mint Yeast Dough**, *page 26. Make up your own combinations.*

1½ tsp. walnut or olive oil
¼ cup chopped walnuts or pine nuts
4 oz. cream cheese, softened
1 egg yolk

1 cup (4 oz.) crumbled feta cheese
¼ cup chopped fresh herbs
⅛-¼ tsp. white or black pepper

In a small skillet, heat oil over medium-high heat and sauté nuts for about 2 minutes, stirring frequently. Remove nuts from pan and cool. In a bowl, blend cream cheese with egg yolk. Add feta, herbs, pepper and sautéed nuts and mix until well blended.

SUGGESTED WRAPPERS:
Lemon Mint Yeast Dough, **page 26**
Spinach Yeast Dough, **page 28**
Basic Savory Pastry Dough, **page 36**

Basic Sweet Pastry Dough, **page 37**
Puff Pastry, **page 53**

CHEESY HERB FILLING

Makes about 1¼ cups

*Use chopped fresh cilantro or basil. Some exciting combinations are: cilantro with **Mexican Yeast Dough**, page 21, or basil with **Tomato Basil Yeast Dough**, page 22, or **Onion Yeast Dough**, page 25.*

½ cup ricotta cheese
1 egg yolk
½ cup (2 oz.) grated mozzarella cheese
½ cup (2 oz.) grated sharp cheddar cheese
2 tbs. chopped fresh herbs
¼ tsp. coarsely ground pepper

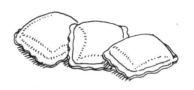

In a bowl, blend ricotta cheese with egg yolk. Add remaining ingredients and mix until well blended.

SUGGESTED WRAPPERS:

Mexican Yeast Dough, page 21
Tomato Basil Yeast Dough, page 22
Onion Yeast Dough, page 25
Tortilla Dough, page 44

Egg Pasta Dough, page 46
Pie Crust, page 52
Puff Pastry, page 53

TUNISIAN CHEESE FILLING

Makes about 1¼ cups

*Tunisian briks are usually made from egg and cheese or meat mixtures, which are wrapped in phyllo and deep fat-fried. I use only the cheese, nuts and seasonings in this loose adaptation. Pine nuts are cheapest if purchased in bulk. I order them from mail order catalogs (see **Sources**, page 150). Walnuts can be substituted for a good, and less expensive, alternative. For an Italian flavor, substitute 2 cups (8 oz.) grated mozzarella cheese for the goat cheese.*

1 tbs. olive oil
¼ cup chopped pine nuts
½ cup (2 oz.) freshly grated
   Parmesan cheese

2 cups (8 oz.) crumbled goat cheese
1 egg yolk
2-3 green onions, thinly sliced
⅛-¼ tsp. white pepper

In a large skillet, heat oil over medium-high heat and sauté pine nuts for about 2 minutes, stirring frequently. Remove from pan and cool. In a bowl, blend cheeses with egg yolk. Add sautéed nuts and remaining ingredients and mix until well blended.

SUGGESTED WRAPPERS:
Spinach Yeast Dough, page 28
Basic Savory Pastry Dough, page 36
Egg Pasta Dough, page 46

Pie Crust, page 52
Puff Pastry, page 53
Phyllo, page 54

CHEESE CALZONE FILLING

Makes about 1½ cups

Pockets made with this filling are are guaranteed to disappear quickly. Serve them as appetizers or as part of a buffet. Virtually any dough can be used. For a variation, add ¼ to ⅓ cup chopped prosciutto or salami.

½ cup ricotta cheese
1 egg yolk
¼ cup (1 oz.) freshly grated Parmesan cheese
1 cup (4 oz.) grated mozzarella cheese
⅛ tsp. salt
¼ tsp. white pepper

In a bowl, blend ricotta cheese with egg yolk. Add remaining ingredients and mix until well blended.

SUGGESTED WRAPPERS:
Rye Yeast Dough, page 19
Garlic Herb Yeast Dough, page 24
Parmesan Pepper Yeast Dough, page 27
Spinach Yeast Dough, page 28

Basic Savory Pastry Dough, page 36
Basic Sweet Pastry Dough, page 37
Pie Crust, page 52
Pizza Crust, page 60

CHEESE PIZZA FILLING

Use your favorite homemade or purchased pizza sauce for this favorite filling. Freeze the unbaked pockets for quick and easy pizza pockets anytime.

½ cup ricotta cheese
1 egg yolk
½ cup (2 oz.) grated mozzarella cheese
2 tbs. freshly grated Parmesan cheese
¼ cup pizza sauce, or to taste

In a bowl, blend ricotta cheese with egg yolk. Add mozzarella and Parmesan and mix until well blended. Spread a small amount of pizza sauce on the inside of each pocket and top with cheese mixture.

SUGGESTED WRAPPERS:
Tomato Basil Yeast Dough, page 22
Parmesan Pepper Yeast Dough, page 27
Egg Pasta Dough, page 46
Pie Crust, page 52
Pizza Crust, page 60

WHITE PIZZA FILLING

Makes about 1½ cups

Based on an Italian recipe for "pizza bianca," this classic combination will complement any meal or stand alone as a meal with a salad.

½ cup ricotta cheese
1 egg yolk
½ cup (2 oz.) grated provolone cheese
½ cup (2 oz.) grated mozzarella cheese
⅛-¼ tsp. white pepper

In a bowl, blend ricotta cheese with egg yolk. Add remaining ingredients and mix until well blended.

SUGGESTED WRAPPERS:

Tomato Basil Yeast Dough, page 22
Parmesan Pepper Yeast Dough, page 27
Egg Pasta Dough, page 46

Pie Crust, page 52
Pizza Crust, page 60

THREE CHEESE FILLING

The paprika provides flavoring as well as color and can be adjusted to taste.

1 egg yolk
1 cup (4 oz.) grated cheddar cheese
¼ cup (1 oz.) grated mozzarella cheese
¼ cup (1 oz.) grated Emmentaler or Swiss cheese
¼ tsp. salt
½-1 tsp. paprika

In a bowl, beat egg yolk. Stir in cheeses. Add seasonings and mix until well blended.

SUGGESTED WRAPPERS:
Mexican Yeast Dough, page 21
Onion Yeast Dough, page 25
Basic Savory Pastry Dough, page 36

Pie Crust, page 52
Pizza Crust, page 60

MIDDLE EASTERN
THREE CHEESE FILLING

This combination of cheeses and seasonings can be found all over the Middle East, and is used in a variety of ways. If you can find kasseri cheese, use it instead of cheddar for authentic flavor. The herbs can be adjusted to taste. Fresh parsley is easy to find (and inexpensive) in the produce section of any grocery store and gives this filling just the right texture and flavor.

¼ cup ricotta cheese
1 egg yolk
1 cup (4 oz.) crumbled feta cheese
½ cup (2 oz.) grated cheddar cheese
¼ tsp. coarsely ground pepper

1 tbs. chopped fresh parsley, or 1 tsp. dried, crushed
1½ tsp. chopped fresh dill, or ½ tsp. dried, crushed

In a bowl, blend ricotta cheese with egg yolk. Add remaining ingredients and mix until well blended.

SUGGESTED WRAPPERS:
Garlic Herb Yeast Dough, page 24
Parmesan Pepper Yeast Dough, page 27
Egg Pasta Dough, page 46

Pie Crust, page 52
Pizza Crust, page 60

POTATO CHEESE FILLING

Makes about 1¼ cups

You can use leftover mashed potatoes, but if they have already been seasoned, omit the salt and pepper in this recipe. Use a good-quality, sharp cheddar cheese.

1 tbs. olive oil
¼ cup minced onion
½ cup (2 oz.) grated cheddar cheese
½ cup mashed potatoes
¼ tsp. salt
½ tsp. coarsely ground pepper

In a medium skillet, heat oil over medium heat and sauté onion until golden and soft, about 3 to 5 minutes. Remove from heat and cool slightly. Mix all ingredients until well blended.

SUGGESTED WRAPPERS:
Rye Yeast Dough, page 19
Garlic Herb Yeast Dough with dill, page 24
Onion Yeast Dough, page 25
Basic Savory Pastry Dough, page 36

Tortilla Dough, page 44
Chapati Dough, page 49
Pizza Crust, page 60

INDIAN POTATO FILLING

Makes about 1½ cups

In India, potatoes are frequently used as a filling for pockets, mixed with native seasonings. Use fresh cilantro for this delightful filling, as the dried variety just doesn't provide the same flavor. Leftovers can be enjoyed as a side dish with meat. It's a great alternative to plain mashed potatoes.

2 medium baking potatoes
  (about 1 lb.), cooked, peeled
2 tbs. olive oil
2 tsp. lime juice
2 tbs. chopped fresh cilantro
1 tbs. minced onion

½ tsp. grated ginger root
1 clove garlic, minced
¼ tsp. salt
¼ tsp. ground cumin
¼-½ tsp. cayenne pepper

With an electric mixer, briefly blend potatoes with olive oil and lime juice until smooth, but not gummy. Add remaining ingredients and mix with a spoon until well blended.

SUGGESTED WRAPPERS:
Whole Wheat Yeast Dough, page 20
Indian Yogurt Dough, page 42
Tortilla Dough, page 44

Chapati Dough, page 49
Pie Crust, page 52
Pizza Crust, page 60

TOMATO RICE FILLING

Makes about 1¼ cups

This recipe is based on Middle Eastern rice fillings that are traditionally wrapped in grape leaves. Use your favorite homemade or purchased pasta sauce.

1 cup cooked rice
¼ cup tomato pasta sauce
1 tbs. chopped fresh parsley, or 1 tsp. dried, crushed
1 tbs. chopped fresh mint, or 1 tsp. dried, crushed
¼ tsp. salt
¼-½ tsp. coarsely ground pepper

Mix all ingredients together until well blended.

SUGGESTED WRAPPERS:
Onion Yeast Dough, **page 25**
Lemon Mint Yeast Dough, **page 26**
Chapati Dough, **page 49**

Pie Crust, **page 52**
Flour Tortillas, **page 59**

MOZZARELLA, TOMATO AND BASIL FILLING

This classic combination is sure to please. If using nuts, heat 1½ tsp. walnut or olive oil in a small skillet and sauté the nuts over medium-high heat for about 2 minutes, stirring constantly. Cool before adding to the cheese. If desired, add about ¼ cup finely diced proscuitto.

2 medium-sized plum tomatoes
1 clove garlic, minced
1 cup (4 oz.) grated mozzarella cheese
¼ tsp. coarsely ground pepper

2 tbs. chopped fresh basil, or 2 tsp. dried, crushed
2 tbs. chopped toasted walnuts, optional

With a sharp knife, remove the top portion of each tomato and squeeze out seeds and juice. Coarsely chop tomatoes and drain any excess juice. Combine with remaining ingredients and mix until well blended.

SUGGESTED WRAPPERS:
Tomato Basil Yeast Dough, page 22
Parmesan Pepper Yeast Dough, page 27
Basic Savory Pastry Dough, page 36

Pie Crust, page 52
Pizza Crust, page 60

SPICY TOMATO CHEESE FILLING

Makes about 1½ cups

If you use pepper Jack (Monterey Jack cheese flavored with jalapeño peppers) you can omit the jalapeños in this recipe. Any of your favorite hot peppers can be substituted for jalapeños, or use ½ to 1 tsp. crushed red pepper flakes.

2 medium-sized plum tomatoes
½ cup (2 oz.) grated Monterey Jack cheese
½ cup (2 oz.) grated cheddar cheese
½-1 jalapeño pepper, finely diced
2 tbs. minced onion

With a sharp knife, remove the top portion of each tomato and squeeze out seeds and juice. Coarsely chop tomatoes and drain any excess juice. Combine with remaining ingredients and mix until well blended.

SUGGESTED WRAPPERS:
Mexican Yeast Dough, page 21
Garlic Herb Yeast Dough
  with cilantro, page 24

Pie Crust, page 52
Flour Tortillas, page 59
Pizza Crust, page 60

SPANAKOPITA FILLING

Makes about 1 cup

Spanakopita is a traditional savory Greek pie with a filling of spinach and feta cheese and a top and bottom crust made from phyllo. Instead, shape it into triangle-shaped pockets for frying or baking. If desired, substitute ½ cup grated provolone cheese for the feta.

1 pkg. (10 oz.) frozen chopped spinach, thawed
1 tbs. olive oil
2 cloves garlic, minced
½ cup (4 oz.) crumbled feta cheese
½ cup (4 oz.) grated mozzarella cheese

Drain spinach well and squeeze dry. In a large skillet, heat oil over medium-high heat and sauté spinach and garlic until spinach is warm, about 3 minutes. Remove from heat, drain well and cool slightly. Add cheeses and mix until well blended.

SUGGESTED WRAPPERS:
Garlic Yeast Dough, page 23
Lemon Mint Yeast Dough, page 26
Basic Savory Pastry Dough, page 36
Lemon Poppy Seed Pastry Dough, page 39

Puff Pastry, page 53
Phyllo, page 54
Pizza Crust, page 60

QUESADILLA FILLING

If available, use a combination of red, yellow and green bell peppers for color.

1 medium-sized plum tomato
1 tbs. olive oil
1 tbs. minced onion
1 clove garlic, minced
½ cup diced bell pepper
½ cup (2 oz.) grated sharp
   cheddar cheese

½ cup (2 oz.) grated Monterey Jack
   cheese
½ tsp. diced jalapeño pepper, or to
   taste, optional
¼ cup chopped fresh cilantro, or
   to taste

With a sharp knife, remove the top portion of tomato and squeeze out seeds and juice. Coarsely chop tomato and drain any excess juice; set aside. In a medium skillet, heat oil over medium heat and sauté onion, garlic and bell pepper until vegetables are just starting to soften, about 3 to 4 minutes. Add tomato and sauté for 1 to 2 minutes. Remove from heat, drain well and cool slightly. Add remaining ingredients and mix until well blended.

SUGGESTED WRAPPERS:
Mexican Yeast Dough, page 21
Tortilla Dough, page 44
Pie Crust, page 52

Flour Tortillas, page 59
Pizza Crust, page 60

MUSHROOM FILLING

This makes a wonderful low-fat pocket, especially when using a yeast dough.

4 oz. fresh mushrooms
1 tbs. olive oil
¼ cup minced onion
2 cloves garlic, minced
salt to taste
freshly ground pepper to taste
2 tbs. chopped fresh parsley, or 2 tsp. dried, crushed

Process mushrooms briefly with a food processor until coarsely chopped. In a large skillet, heat olive oil over medium-high heat and sauté mushrooms, onions and garlic until mushrooms are tender and onion is soft, about 3 to 4 minutes. Add parsley, salt and pepper and sauté for 1 to 2 minutes. Cool slightly.

SUGGESTED WRAPPERS:
Garlic Yeast Dough, page 23
Parmesan Pepper Yeast Dough
   with parsley, page 27
Basic Savory Pastry Dough, page 36

Tortilla Dough, page 44
Chapati Dough, page 49
Pie Crust, page 52
Pizza Crust, page 60

MUSHROOM AND CHEESE FILLING

Makes about 1¼ cups

This is a flavorful, relatively low-fat filling that goes best with a flavored yeast dough to keep the calories down.

1 tbs. olive oil
4 oz. fresh mushrooms
1 clove garlic, minced
½ cup low-fat cottage cheese
1 tsp. dried dill weed, crushed

Chop mushrooms coarsely, or process mushrooms briefly with a food processor until coarsely chopped. In a large skillet, heat oil over medium-high heat and sauté mushrooms and garlic until mushrooms are tender, about 3 to 4 minutes. Cool slightly. Add remaining ingredients and mix until well blended.

SUGGESTED WRAPPERS:
Garlic Herb Yeast Dough with dill, page 24
Parmesan Pepper Yeast Dough, page 27
Spinach Yeast Dough, page 28

Flour Tortillas, page 59
Pizza Crust, page 60

BROCCOLI CHEDDAR FILLING

Makes about 1½ cups

This is for broccoli lovers. The recipe calls for just enough cheese to flavor, but not to overwhelm.

1 pkg. (10 oz.) frozen chopped broccoli
1 cup (4 oz.) grated cheddar cheese
1-2 tbs. minced onion, optional
¼ tsp. salt
⅛-¼ tsp. cayenne pepper

Cook broccoli according to package directions until tender-crisp, about ¾ of the recommended cooking time. Drain broccoli very well and cool slightly. Add remaining ingredients and mix until well blended.

SUGGESTED WRAPPERS:
Potato Yeast Dough, page 18
Rye Yeast Dough, page 19
Onion Yeast Dough, page 25
Chapati Dough, page 49

Pie Crust, page 52
Flour Tortillas, page 59
Pizza Crust, page 60

BEAN BRIK FILLING

Makes about 2 cups

This flavorful filling is based on a Tunisian recipe for a deep-fried turnover. It's a favorite of vegetarians and meat-lovers alike.

2 medium-sized plum tomatoes
1 can (15½ oz.) kidney beans, rinsed, drained
1 small baking potato (about 3 oz.) cooked, peeled, diced
¼ cup grated carrot
2 green onions, chopped
2 cloves garlic, minced

¼ tsp. salt
½ tsp. coarsely ground pepper
¼ tsp. ground cumin
¼ tsp. ground coriander
¼ tsp. crushed red pepper flakes
½ tsp. caraway seeds
1½ tsp. lemon juice

With a sharp knife, remove the top portion of each tomato and squeeze out seeds and juice. Quarter tomatoes and place in the workbowl of a food processor with beans. Pulse until coarsely chopped. Add remaining ingredients and process until just blended.

SUGGESTED WRAPPERS:
Potato Yeast Dough, page 18
Rye Yeast Dough, page 19
Garlic Yeast Dough, page 23
Basic Savory Pastry Dough, page 36

Basic Sweet Pastry Dough, page 37
Chapati Dough, page 49
Pie Crust, page 52

SOUTHWESTERN
BLACK BEAN FILLING

This is for those of you who love black beans. It's guaranteed to receive rave reviews. If there are any leftovers, try using this filling as a dip for chips.

1 can (15.5 oz.) black beans, rinsed, drained
1 tsp. chopped jalapeño pepper, or to taste
¼ cup minced onion
1 clove garlic, minced
2 tbs. sour cream
½ cup grated Monterey Jack cheese
¼ tsp. salt
1 tbs. chopped fresh cilantro

Puree beans with a food processor. Add remaining ingredients and process until well blended.

SUGGESTED WRAPPERS:
Mexican Yeast Dough, page 21
Tortilla Dough, page 44

Chapati Dough, page 49
Pie Crust, page 52

GEORGIAN BEAN FILLING

Makes about 1½ cups

If you like cilantro, you'll love this filling. Any type of bean can be used — use your favorite. If there is any filling left, mix it into hot cooked rice or scrambled eggs, or spread it on crackers.

1½ tsp. olive or vegetable oil
¼ cup minced red onion
1 clove garlic, minced
1 can (15½ oz.) kidney beans,
   rinsed, drained
¼ tsp. salt

¼-½ tsp. crushed red pepper flakes
½ cup chopped fresh cilantro,
   or to taste
1 cup (4 oz.) grated sharp cheddar
   cheese

In a medium skillet, heat oil over medium heat and sauté onion and garlic until soft and golden, about 3 to 5 minutes; cool. Puree beans with a food processor. Add salt, pepper flakes and cilantro and process until well blended. Add cheese, onion and garlic and process until well blended.

SUGGESTED WRAPPERS:
Onion Yeast Dough, **page 25**
Basic Savory Pastry Dough, **page 36**
Tortilla Dough, **page 44**
Chinese Dumpling Dough, **page 48**

Chapati Dough, **page 49**
Egg Roll Wrappers, **page 56**
Flour Tortillas, **page 59**

SWEET FILLINGS

APPLE FILLING

Makes about 1¼ cups

Processing the apples with a food processor makes this flavorful apple filling easy to make. If you enjoy a slice of sharp cheddar cheese on apple pie, top the filling with a small amount of cheddar cheese before sealing the pocket. Use Golden Delicious, Granny Smith, McIntosh, Newton, Pippin or Rome Beauty apples. The more tart the apples, the more sugar you will need.

2 medium apples
1 tsp. lemon juice
2-3 tbs. sugar
2 tbs. chopped walnuts, optional
¼ cup raisins, optional

Peel, core and quarter apples. Place apples in the workbowl of a food processor with lemon juice and process until finely chopped. Add sugar and walnuts and raisins, if using, and pulse until just blended.

SUGGESTED WRAPPERS:
Basic Savory Yeast Dough, page 16
Basic Sweet Yeast Dough, page 17
Basic Savory Pastry Dough, page 36
Basic Sweet Pastry Dough, page 37
Pie Crust, page 52

CRANBERRY FILLING

Makes about ½ cup

*This makes a great breakfast or dessert pocket, especially in the fall or during the winter holidays. If you're serving several flavors of pockets on a buffet, this goes well with **Tropical Nut Filling**, page 136, or any of the **Basic Cream Cheese Fillings** on pages 144 to 148.*

1½ cups whole cranberries
½ cup sugar
1 tsp. grated orange peel

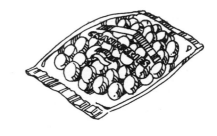

Process cranberries with a food processor until finely chopped. Place in a medium saucepan with sugar and orange peel and bring to a boil over medium-high heat. Reduce heat to low and simmer until mixture thickens, stirring constantly. Cool.

SUGGESTED WRAPPERS:
***Orange Ginger Yeast Dough**, page 29*
***Basic Sweet Pastry Dough**, page 37*
Cream Cheese Pastry Dough
    with orange peel, page 41

***Pie Crust**, page 52*
***Puff Pastry**, page 53*

LEMON CREAM FILLING

This classic lemon cream Danish filling also makes great pockets. Seal the dough very tightly. There may be a little leaking, but the resulting flavor is well worth the trouble it takes to clean up the mess.

4 egg yolks
½ cup sugar
¼ cup lemon juice

1 tsp. grated lemon peel
3 tbs. half-and-half
5 tbs. butter or margarine

In a medium saucepan, beat egg yolks with sugar. Add lemon juice, lemon peel and half-and-half and mix well. Add butter. Cook over medium heat, stirring constantly, until mixture thickens, about 10 minutes. Remove from heat, pour mixture into a heat-resistant container and cool completely.

SUGGESTED WRAPPERS:
Lemon Mint Yeast Dough, page 26
Coconut Ginger Pastry Dough, page 38
Lemon Poppy Seed Pastry Dough, page 39

Cream Cheese Pastry Dough
with lemon peel, page 41
Pie Crust, page 52

COCONUT CREAM FILLING

Seal the dough tightly to prevent leaks in the filled pockets.

1½ cups sweetened flaked coconut
¼ cup sugar
1 tbs. all-purpose flour
⅔ cup half-and-half

2 tbs. butter or margarine
1 tsp. coconut extract
2 egg yolks

In a medium saucepan, combine coconut, sugar, flour and half-and-half. Cook over medium-low heat, stirring frequently, until mixture thickens, about 6 to 10 minutes. Add butter and cook, stirring, until butter melts and is incorporated into the mixture, about 1 minute. Reduce heat to low, add extract and yolks. Mix until well blended and cook for 1 minute. Remove from heat, pour mixture into a heat-resistant container and cool completely.

SUGGESTED WRAPPERS:
Lemon Mint Yeast Dough, page 26
Orange Ginger Yeast Dough, page 29
Basic Sweet Pastry Dough
  with lemon peel, page 37

Lemon Poppy Seed Pastry Dough, page 39
Pie Crust, page 52

NUT FILLING

Pecans can be substituted for walnuts if you have an abundance. Allspice, nutmeg or mace can be used instead of cinnamon. Variations on this simple nut filling are eaten all over the world.

1 cup chopped walnuts
¼ cup sugar
1 tbs. cinnamon
2 tbs. cream or half-and-half

Process nuts, sugar and cinnamon with a food processor until very finely ground, taking care not to overprocess to a paste. Add cream and pulse until just mixed.

SUGGESTED WRAPPERS:
Orange Ginger Yeast Dough, **page 29**   *Crescent Rolls,* **page 58**
Cream Cheese Pastry Dough, **page 41**

ALMOND FILLING

Pockets made from this filling are delicious for breakfast, brunch or dessert with coffee. Use chopped macadamia nuts as a substitute for almonds.

³⁄₄ cup sliced almonds
2 tbs. butter or margarine, softened
¹⁄₂ tsp. almond extract
¹⁄₄ cup brown sugar, packed

Process almonds with a food processor until finely chopped; set aside. With an electric mixer, blend butter with extract and sugar. Add nuts and mix until well blended.

SUGGESTED WRAPPERS:
Orange Ginger Yeast Dough, page 29   *Pie Crust*, page 52
Cream Cheese Pastry Dough, page 41

CHOCOLATE NUT FILLING

Makes about 1¼ cups

This is for chocoholics. Use your favorite type of nuts. Make 3- or 4-inch pockets with this filling.

¼ cup butter or margarine, softened
¼ cup cocoa powder

½ cup sugar
½ cup finely chopped nuts

With an electric mixer, blend butter with cocoa and sugar. Add nuts and mix until well blended.

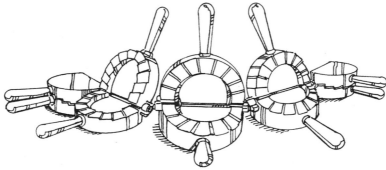

SUGGESTED WRAPPERS:
Basic Sweet Yeast Dough, page 17
Coconut Ginger Pastry Dough, page 38

Pie Crust, page 52

RAISIN NUT FILLING

Any nut can be substituted as can any dried fruit. When finely chopped, the raisins or dried fruit serve as a nonfat binder for the filling.

1 cup walnut pieces
½ cup raisins or chopped dried fruit
1 tsp. cinnamon

Process all ingredients with a food processor until finely chopped and well blended.

SUGGESTED WRAPPERS:
***Potato Yeast Dough*, page 18**   ***Pie Crust*, page 52**
***Vienna Pastry Dough*, page 40**

TROPICAL NUT FILLING

Makes about 1 cup

This filling combines wonderful flavors for a tropical sensation. The ingredients are processed in batches to chop them uniformly.

½ cup Brazil nuts
3 oz. dried apricots (about 20-25, depending on size)
½ tsp. grated ginger root
¼ cup sweetened flaked coconut
1 tsp. grated orange peel

In batches, process all ingredients with a food processor until coarsely chopped. Add all ingredients to the workbowl and process until finely chopped and well blended.

SUGGESTED WRAPPERS:
Orange Ginger Yeast Dough, page 29
Coconut Ginger Pastry Dough, page 38
Lemon Poppy Seed Pastry Dough, page 39
Pie Crust, page 52

POPPY SEED NUT FILLING

Makes about ¾ cup

*To save money, buy poppy seeds in bulk at gourmet shops or through mail order catalogs (see **Sources**, page 150). Spray a measuring spoon with nonstick spray before measuring the honey — it will slide right off. The recipe can be easily doubled if desired.*

¼ cup butter or margarine, softened
2 tbs. honey
¼ cup poppy seeds
½ cup finely chopped walnuts

Process all ingredients with a food processor until well blended.

SUGGESTED WRAPPERS:
Lemon Mint Yeast Dough, **page 26**   *Pie Crust*, **page 52**
Lemon Poppy Seed Pastry Dough, **page 39**   *Puff Pastry*, **page 53**
Cream Cheese Pastry Dough
   with lemon peel, page 41

PUMPKIN WALNUT FILLING

Makes about 1¼ cups

For a real holiday treat, add about ¼ cup dried sweetened cranberries. They're sometimes called "craisins" or "crannies."

1 cup canned pumpkin
½-1 tsp. pumpkin pie spice or apple pie spice
¼ cup brown sugar, packed
¼ cup chopped walnuts

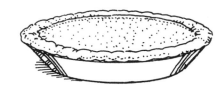

Mix all ingredients until well blended.

SUGGESTED WRAPPERS:
Basic Sweet Yeast Dough, page 17
Vienna Pastry Dough, page 40

Cream Cheese Pastry Dough, page 41
Pie Crust, page 52

CANDIED FRUIT FILLING

Makes about 1 cup

This recipe is based on a Greek confection. Candied fruit is easy to find in grocery stores in the fall or during the holiday season. It is usually used for fruitcakes. Even if you don't like fruitcake, you'll love this filling.

½ cup chopped walnuts or pecans
½ cup candied fruit
½ cup orange marmalade

Process nuts and candied fruit with a food processor until coarsely chopped. Add marmalade and process briefly until just blended.

SUGGESTED WRAPPERS:
Orange Ginger Yeast Dough, page 29
Cream Cheese Pastry Dough, page 41

Pie Crust, page 52
Crescent Rolls, page 58

ALMOND APRICOT FILLING

Makes about 1 cup

Almonds and apricots complement each other perfectly. Processing the apricots with flour prevents the apricots from forming a solid mass. The flour also helps to thicken the filling.

6 oz. dried apricots (about 40-50, depending on size)
1 tbs. all-purpose flour
½ cup orange juice
1 tbs. lemon juice
½ cup chopped or sliced almonds

Process apricots and flour with a food processor until apricots are finely chopped. Place mixture in a medium saucepan with orange juice and cook over medium heat, stirring constantly, until mixture thickens, about 5 minutes. Remove from heat and stir in lemon juice and nuts. Cool.

SUGGESTED WRAPPERS:
Basic Sweet Yeast Dough, page 17
Orange Ginger Yeast Dough, page 29
Basic Sweet Pastry Dough, page 37

Cream Cheese Pastry Dough
with orange peel, page 41
Puff Pastry, page 53

SOUTH AMERICAN RAISIN-CHEESE FILLING

Raisins are a common ingredient in South American cooking. For a twist, use dried, sweetened cranberries (craisins), cherries or blueberries in this sweet cheese filling.

¼ cup raisins
2 hard-cooked eggs
1½ tsp. sugar
1 cup grated mozzarella cheese

Process all ingredients with a food processor until finely chopped and well blended.

SUGGESTED WRAPPERS:
***Basic Sweet Yeast Dough*, page 17**   ***Pie Crust*, page 52**
***Basic Sweet Pastry Dough*, page 37**

SWEET CHEESE FILLING

This filling makes wonderful breakfast or dessert turnovers. Substitute 1 to 2 tsp. cinnamon for the grated peel if desired.

4 oz. cream cheese, softened
1 egg yolk
1/4 cup confectioners' sugar
1 tbs. grated lemon or orange peel
1 cup ricotta cheese
1/4 tsp. salt

With an electric mixer, blend cream cheese with egg yolk. Blend in sugar and lemon peel. Add ricotta cheese and salt and mix until well blended.

SUGGESTED WRAPPERS:
Orange Ginger Yeast Dough, page 29
Lemon Poppy Seed Pastry Dough, page 39
Vienna Pastry Dough, page 40
Pie Crust, page 52
Puff Pastry, page 53

GREEK HONEY CHEESE FILLING

Makes about 1 cup

Make sure to seal turnovers tightly to avoid leaking. This sweet filling is sure to please. It's adapted from a Greek recipe for honey pie (Melopita).

1 cup ricotta cheese
¼ cup honey
1 tbs. sugar
1 egg yolk
½ tsp. lemon juice
½ tsp. cinnamon

In a large bowl, beat ricotta cheese until smooth. Blend in honey and sugar. Add egg yolk, lemon juice and cinnamon and mix until well blended.

SUGGESTED WRAPPERS:
***Lemon Mint Yeast Dough*, page 26**
Basic Sweet Pastry Dough
   with lemon peel, page 37

***Lemon Poppy Seed Pastry Dough*, page 39**
***Pie Crust*, page 52**

ABOUT BASIC CREAM CHEESE FILLINGS

The following recipes, which use cream cheese as the basic ingredient, are flavorful and easy to make.

- Use regular, light or nonfat cream cheese. Soften it at room temperature before using.

- Both yeast dough wrappers and pastry dough wrappers work well with cream cheese fillings. Avoid using pastry made with cream cheese or your pockets will be almost too rich to eat.

- If serving pockets with a special coffee or on a buffet, make varieties with several different, complementary fillings.

- The recipes can be easily halved if making a variety.

- Make quick and easy cream cheese fillings with items already on hand in your refrigerator. For example, mix 2 to 4 tablespoons of your favorite fruit spread with 8 ounces cream cheese. Enclose the filling in one of the *Ready-Made Wrappers*, pages 51-60. Lemon curd and guava jelly are especially delicious with cream cheese. Savory cream cheese pockets can be made with mango chutney or jalapeño jelly.

CREAM CHEESE NUT FILLING

Makes about 1½ cups

Virtually any nut could be used, although walnuts, pecans or almonds are the most common. If using almonds, you can substitute almond extract for vanilla.

8 oz. cream cheese, softened
1 cup confectioners' sugar

1 tsp. vanilla extract
1 cup finely chopped nuts

With an electric mixer, blend cream cheese with confectioners' sugar. Add remaining ingredients and mix until well blended.

VARIATION: CREAM CHEESE COCONUT FILLING

Substitute 2 tsp. coconut extract for vanilla extract and ½ cup sweetened flaked coconut for the almonds.

SUGGESTED WRAPPERS:
Basic Sweet Yeast Dough, page 17
Orange Ginger Yeast Dough, page 29
Coconut Ginger Pastry Dough, page 38
Lemon Poppy Seed Pastry Dough, page 39
Puff Pastry, page 53

CREAM CHEESE
FRUIT AND NUT FILLING

Makes about 1 cup

Use your favorite nuts, such as pecans, walnuts, almonds or pistachio nuts. Dried blueberries, cherries or cranberries are wonderful alternatives to raisins.

8 oz. cream cheese, softened
1/2 cup confectioners' sugar
1/2 cup finely chopped nuts
1/4 cup raisins or chopped dried fruit
1/2-1 tsp. grated orange or lemon peel

With an electric mixer, blend cream cheese with confectioners' sugar. Add remaining ingredients and mix until well blended.

SUGGESTED WRAPPERS:
Lemon Mint Yeast Dough, page 26   ***Pie Crust***, page 52
Coconut Ginger Pastry Dough, page 38

CREAM CHEESE
CITRUS-ALMOND FILLING

If using freshly grated orange or lemon peel (zest), strip the peel of 1 medium lemon or 1 small orange directly into the mixing bowl.

8 oz. cream cheese, softened
1/2 cup confectioners' sugar
2 tsp. orange or lemon extract

2 tbs. grated orange or lemon peel
1/4 cup sliced or chopped almonds

With an electric mixer, blend cream cheese with confectioners' sugar. Add remaining ingredients and mix until well blended.

SUGGESTED WRAPPERS:
Lemon Mint Yeast Dough, **page 26**
Orange Ginger Yeast Dough, **page 29**
Basic Sweet Pastry Dough, **page 37**
Lemon Poppy Seed Pastry Dough, **page 39**
Pie Crust, **page 52**

TROPICAL CREAM CHEESE FILLING

Makes about 1½ cups

The combination of exotic flavors in this filling is out of this world.

8 oz. cream cheese, softened
½ cup orange or peach preserves
½ cup sweetened flaked coconut
1 tsp. grated ginger root
½ cup sliced almonds or chopped macadamia nuts

With an electric mixer, blend cream cheese with confectioners' sugar. Add remaining ingredients and mix until well blended.

SUGGESTED WRAPPERS:
Orange Ginger Yeast Dough, page 29
Coconut Ginger Pastry Dough, page 38

Lemon Poppy Seed Pastry Dough, page 39
Pie Crust, page 52

CREAM CHEESE DATE FILLING

Makes about 1½ cups

If you can't find chopped dates in the grocery store, process about 20 whole dates and the sugar with a food processor until coarsely chopped. The sugar will coat the dates and prevent a sticky mess. This is a very sweet filling. For a delicious variation, add 1 tsp. almond extract and ¼ cup chopped walnuts.

8 oz. chopped dates
3 tbs. sugar
1-2 tsp. grated orange peel
8 oz. cream cheese, softened

Process dates, sugar and orange peel with a food processor until finely chopped. Add cream cheese and process until well blended.

SUGGESTED WRAPPERS:
Basic Sweet Yeast Dough, page 17   **Pie Crust, page 52**
Basic Sweet Pastry Dough, page 37

SOURCES

POCKET MAKERS

Easy Pockets
Southampton, NY
(516) 283-4700 or (800) 221-1688

The Pampered Chef, Ltd.
Addison, IL
(630) 261-8900 or (800) 226-5562

VillaWare
Cleveland, OH
(800) 822-1335

Progressive International
Kent, WA
(800) 426-7101

BULK SPICES, SEEDS AND NUTS

Penderey's
Dallas, TX
(800) 533-1870

Penzey's Spice House
Waukesha, WI
(414) 574-0277

The Spice House
Milwaukee, WI
(414) 272-0977

INDEX

SERVE CREATIVE, EASY, NUTRITIOUS MEALS WITH nitty gritty® COOKBOOKS

Edible Pockets for Every Meal
Cooking With Chile Peppers
Oven and Rotisserie Roasting
Risottos, Paellas and Other Rice
   Specialties
Entrées From Your Bread Machine
Muffins, Nut Breads and More
Healthy Snacks for Kids
100 Dynamite Desserts
Recipes for Yogurt Cheese
Sautés
Cooking in Porcelain
Appetizers
Casseroles
The Best Bagels are made at home*
   (*perfect for your bread machine)
The Toaster Oven Cookbook
Skewer Cooking on the Grill
Creative Mexican Cooking
Extra-Special Crockery Pot Recipes
Slow Cooking
Cooking in Clay
Marinades
Deep Fried Indulgences

Cooking with Parchment Paper
The Garlic Cookbook
From Your Ice Cream Maker
Cappuccino/Espresso: The Book of
   Beverages
The Best Pizza is made at home*
   (*perfect for your bread machine)
The Well Dressed Potato
Convection Oven Cookery
The Steamer Cookbook
The Pasta Machine Cookbook
The Versatile Rice Cooker
The Dehydrator Cookbook
The Bread Machine Cookbook
The Bread Machine Cookbook II
The Bread Machine Cookbook III
The Bread Machine Cookbook IV:
   Whole Grains and Natural Sugars
The Bread Machine Cookbook V:
   Favorite Recipes from 100 Kitchens
The Bread Machine Cookbook VI:
   *Hand-Shaped Breads from the
   Dough Cycle*

Worldwide Sourdoughs From Your
   Bread Machine
Recipes for the Pressure Cooker
The New Blender Book
The Sandwich Maker Cookbook
Waffles
Indoor Grilling
The Coffee Book
The Juicer Books I and II
Bread Baking (traditional)
No Salt, No Sugar, No Fat Cookbook
Cooking for 1 or 2
Quick and Easy Pasta Recipes
The 9x13 Pan Cookbook
Recipes for the Loaf Pan
Low Fat American Favorites
Now That's Italian!
Healthy Cooking on the Run
The Wok
Favorite Seafood Recipes
New International Fondue Cookbook
Favorite Cookie Recipes
Flatbreads From Around the World

For a free catalog, write or call:
Bristol Publishing Enterprises, Inc.
P.O. Box 1737, San Leandro, CA 94577
(800) 346-4889; in California, (510) 895-4461